D1564296

DATE			

Practical Peacemaking
in the Middle East

Practical Peacemaking
in the Middle East

GENERAL EDITOR
Steven L. Spiegel

VOLUME I: *Arms Control and Regional Security*

VOLUME II: *The Environment, Water, Refugees, and Economic
             Cooperation and Development*

A Project of the University of California

IGCC

Institute on Global Conflict and Cooperation

Practical Peacemaking in the Middle East

VOLUME I
Arms Control and Regional Security

Edited by

Steven L. Spiegel
and David J. Pervin

GARLAND PUBLISHING, INC. • NEW YORK & LONDON
1995

Library of Congress Cataloging-in-Publication Data

Practical peacemaking in the Middle East / edited by
Steven L. Spiegel and David J. Pervin.
    v. <1–   > cm.
    "A project of the University of California Institute
on Global Conflict and Cooperation"—V. 1, half t.p.
    "Grew out of international conference held at the
University of California, Los Angeles, in June 1993"—
V. 1, acknowledg.
    Includes index.
    Contents: v. 1. Arms control and regional secu-
rity —
    ISBN 0-8153-1999-1 (v. 1 : alk. paper)
    1. Israel-Arab conflicts—Congresses.   2. Jewish-
Arab relations—Economic aspects—Congresses.
3. Middle East—Economic conditions—1979– —Congresses.   4. Arms control—Middle East—Congresses.
5. Middle East—Military relations—Congresses.
I. Spiegel, Steven L.   II. Pervin, David J.   III. University of California Institute on Global Conflict and Cooperation.
DS119.7.P725   1995
327.5694017'4927—dc20   94-40942
                                                      CIP

Printed on acid-free, 250-year-life paper
Manufactured in the United States of America

To Yehoshafat Harkabi
1922–1994

Contents

PART II

Factors Affecting Arms Control and Regional Security

PART III

Implementation and Verification

PART IV

The Politics and Institutionalization of Regional Security

Figures

Preface

This book is dedicated to the memory of Yehoshafat Harkabi, an early proponent of Arab–Israeli peace and a participant in this project.

Steven L. Spiegel
Los Angeles, California
November, 1994

Acknowledgments

This volume grew out of an international conference held at the University of California, Los Angeles in June 1993. The editors and contributors wish to thank the United States Institute of Peace, which provided the basic grant which made this conference possible; and both the University of California Institute on Global Conflict and Cooperation (IGCC) and the University of California, Los Angeles Center for International Relations (CIR) which provided administrative support and additional financial assistance. In particular, IGCC and CIR directors Susan Shirk and Richard Rosecrance were assiduous in their support and encouragement. We are also especially grateful to Stanley Sheinbaum for his encouragement, guidance, and advice.

The editors wish to thank Deborah Gerner, Brigid Starkey, and Victor LeVine for their comments on early drafts, IGCC Managing Editor Jennifer R. Pournelle for her backing and assistance, and Matthew Maxwell for manuscript preparation. The volume could not have been completed without them. We are also grateful to David Estrin of Garland Publishing for his vision and enthusiasm, which facilitated completion of the task.

Abbreviations

ABACC	Argentine–Brazilian Agency for Accounting and Control of Nuclear Material
ARCS	Arms Control and Regional Security
C^3I	command, control, communications and intelligence
CBMs	confidence-building measures
CEPs	circle of error-probable
CFE	Conventional Forces in Europe
CIR	Center for International Relations
CMC	Cooperative Monitoring Center
CSBMs	Confidence- and Security-Building Measures
CSCE	Conference on Security and Cooperation in Europe
CSCME	Conference on Security and Cooperation in the Middle East
CWC	Chemical Weapons Convention
DFLP	Democratic Front for the Liberation of Palestine
DOP	Declaration of Principles
ECMs	electronic counter measures
EEC	European Economic Community
EU	European Union
EURATOM	European Atomic Energy Community
GRIT	Graduated and Reciprocated Reduction in Tension
GCC	Gulf Cooperation Council
IAEA	International Atomic Energy Agency
IGCC	Institute on Global Conflict and Cooperation
INF	Intermediate Range Nuclear Forces

MASCME	Multilateral Agency for Security and Cooperation in the Middle East
MENWFZ	Middle East Nuclear Weapon Free Zone
MTCR	Missile Technology Control Regime
NACC	North Atlantic Cooperation Council
NPT	Nuclear Non-Proliferation Treaty
NTMs	national technical means
NWFZ	Nuclear Weapon Free Zone
OPANAL	Agency for the Prohibition of Nuclear Weapons in Latin America
PFLP	People's Front for the Liberation of Palestine
PLO	Palestine Liberation Organization
PGMs	precision guided munitions
SCCC	Common System of Accounting and Control of Nuclear Materials
UNDOF	United Nations Disengagement Observers Force
UNEF	United Nations Emergency Force
UNIFIL	United Nations Forces in Lebanon
UNSCRs	United Nations Security Council Resolutions
WEU	Western European Union
WMDFZ	Weapons of Mass Destruction Free Zone

1   Introduction

Steven L. Spiegel and David J. Pervin

In the wake of the breakthroughs in the bilateral negotiations between Israel and, respectively, the Palestine Liberation Organization (PLO) and Jordan, for the first time the interaction between Arabs and Israelis has the potential to be dominated by cooperation rather than conflict. While there has always been an Arab–Israeli dialogue, in the past it was epitomized by rejection and antagonism. Indeed, not only did Arabs and Israelis rarely openly talk with each other, they barely talked *at* each other. Rather, because of the rejection, words and actions were directed either at domestic or extra-regional audiences. This was as true of unofficial and private meetings as it was at the official level.

It is on the symbolic level that the breakthroughs are the most important. Just as the 1977 visit to Israel by President Anwar Sadat of Egypt was crucial to breaking down psychological walls, so, too, the September 1993 Declaration of Principles signed by Israel and the PLO and the October 1994 peace treaty between Israel and Jordan symbolized the end of rejection, the renunciation of the threat or use of force, and the beginning of a process of mutual acceptance. Once that principle was established, the extended interim period of normalization could begin. This stage will be difficult, for there are real conflicts of interest, a high level of suspicion and distrust as a residue of decades of conflict and rejection, and domestic opposition on both sides to the agreements and the peace process.

This breakthrough at the official level was preceded by important dialogues at the unofficial level. Best known of these is the so-called "Oslo channel" that was instrumental in the process leading to the September 1993 Israel–PLO Declaration of Principles. There have also been secret Jordanian–Israeli talks over many years. Since the opening of the Madrid peace process in 1991, there have been many meetings, conferences, and seminars that have brought together Arab, Israeli, and extra-regional participants to discuss a variety of issues of common concern.[1] These meetings have performed the valuable function of creating mutual respect, identifying commonalities, and creating a constituency favoring peace. This dialogue was previously impossible.

BACKGROUND TO THE MADRID PEACE PROCESS

For over 40 years Israel, the Palestinians, and the Arab states were locked in a deeply rooted conflict, one that involved each antagonist's polity, economy, military, and at a basic level society. Intermittent warfare was interspersed with attacks by each side against political and civilian targets of the other. Fear and insecurity were endemic on both the personal and national levels. It was easy, and considered realistic, to assume that what had been would continue to be.

Of course, there were efforts to ameliorate and even resolve the conflict. Both the United States and the Soviet Union at times tried to push a diplomatic peace process. Such efforts were unsuccessful due to procedural and substantive differences between the superpowers which were exploited by the regional states, among whom there was little substantive agreement on the meaning of peace or even of a political settlement. Indeed, the frequent Arab and Israeli proclamations of an interest in peace were usually directed less at one another than at the external powers upon whom they depended. In a situation in which there was no agreement as to the end result, there could be little discussion of how to get from here—a situation of conflict—to there—peace. And with no discussions to bridge differences regarding both outcome and process, there were no practical steps taken by any party that could reassure the others of benign intentions.

The exception to this record of stasis is the Egyptian–Israeli peace treaty of 1979. This agreement, and the process that led up to it, demonstrated three critical building blocks:

1. the importance of a gradual period of acclimatization during which a convergence concerning means and ends develops, i.e., a period of learning.[2] The peace treaty was preceded by an extended period, beginning with the first disengagement of forces agreement in 1974, through the Sinai II agreement of 1975 in which Egypt renounced the use of force, to secret negotiations leading up to President Anwar Sadat's dramatic visit to Jerusalem in 1977, and concluding with the Camp David Accords of 1978 and then the 1979 negotiations over a peace treaty. During this extended period a basis for accommodation developed.[3]

2. the need for direct contacts and for actions to be directed as much at the other side as at outside powers. While this was apparent from the initial negotiations preceding the first disengagement agreement, its most dramatic demonstration came with Egyptian President Anwar Sadat's visit to Jerusalem in 1977.

3. the central role of practical steps that allowed each side to test the intentions of the other and eventually build confidence in the sincerity of the desire for peace.

While the preamble of the Egyptian–Israeli peace treaty saw it as "an important step in the search for comprehensive peace in the area and for the settlement of the Arab–Israeli conflict in all its aspects,"[4] for more than a decade there were no additional steps toward comprehensive peace. During the late 1980s conditions looked propitious. The weakening of the Soviet Union decreased its economic, military and political assistance to its regional allies, in particular Syria, and as Moscow increasingly sought to improve relations with the United States and Israel, it made clear to Damascus that it opposed war.[5] In the wake of the Palestinian *intifada* (uprising) in the Occupied Territories, the Palestine Liberation Organization met American terms and the two briefly entered into a dialogue. The United States undertook considerable diplomatic activity in an effort to convene an international conference as the first step toward comprehensive peace but met with considerable resistance in the region.[6]

Regional war soon replaced peace efforts. In August, 1990, Iraq invaded and occupied Kuwait. The massive American response, concluding with Iraq's devastating defeat and expulsion from Kuwait, increased the credibility of the United States in the region. The need for American intervention also demonstrated the weakness of the regional balance of power and the limited security of countries that, notwithstanding massive investments in military hardware, still had little ability to defend themselves. Iraq's missile attacks on Saudi Arabia and Israel made clear to the Israeli public that in the future, war would not be fought only on the battlefields but would also involve urban civilians. A situation of nascent, or even extant, mutual deterrence thus existed.

The war also increased domestic pressures that threatened political stability in the region, as popular sympathy in the Arab world for Iraq's invasion demonstrated extensive discontent and resentment at inequalities of wealth and the lack of legitimacy of the ruling elite. The threat posed by radical Islamic fundamentalist groups opposed to the status quo within countries and the region accentuated the need to address fundamental social, economic, and even political problems. The challenge posed by the militant Hamas movement to the PLO and Israelis may have been of particular importance.[7] In Israel, the need to integrate the massive influx of immigrants from the former Soviet Union also increased pressure to limit military spending and, specifically, to shift spending away from settlement activity in the occupied West Bank and Gaza Strip.

By 1991, then, a combination of global, regional, and local changes had occurred that increased the receptivity of the regional parties—Israel, Arab States, and the PLO—to a renewed American push for a diplomatic process to resolve the Arab–Israeli conflict. The Soviet Union's demise eliminated an important patron of Syria while increasing the number of immigrants to Israel; the balance of power between Israel and the Arab states made war an unattractive option given the expected high costs and limited benefits; and the need to address economic and political problems had increased. In short, a number of "prerequisites" for a peace process existed, including a military stalemate detrimental to both sides and the absence of superpower competition.[8]

THE MADRID PEACE PROCESS AND THE MULTILATERAL TALKS

Such was the background to the international conference that began on October 31, 1991 in Madrid, Spain. The peace process initiated at Madrid effectively squared the circle, as it was designed to meet the procedural requirements of the various parties. To meet Arab conditions, an international conference co-sponsored by the US and USSR (subsequently Russia) was convened. Attended by the parties directly involved in the Arab–Israeli conflict, other regional parties, and the European Union, to meet Israel's conditions the conference had no independent authority.[9] After plenary statements, bilateral negotiations between Israel and respectively Syria, Lebanon, and a joint Jordan–Palestinian delegation began, focusing on issues separating the parties and terms for peace. These issues are complex, as American Secretary of State James Baker emphasized:

> The parties have made clear that peace by itself is unachievable without a territorial solution and security; that a territorial solution by itself will not resolve the conflict without there also being peace and security; and that security by itself is impossible to achieve without a territorial solution and peace. The process . . . can work only if all issues are put on the table, and if all issues are satisfactorily resolved.[10]

An innovation in the Madrid peace process is the multilateral talks on five issues of regional concern: water, the environment, refugees, economic development, and arms control and regional security. They are based on the premise that because these issues cross boundaries, they require multilateral cooperation and have the potential for providing mutual benefits.[11] In addition, there is a potential for tradeoffs both within and across issues and for positive spill-over into the bilateral negotiations.[12] That is, the multilaterals potentially can serve as a "catalyst for the bilateral talks and progress in the bilateral" negotiations.[13] As former Assistant Secretary of State for Near East Affairs Edward Djerejian pointed out, the multilaterals have "create[d] a web of functional interests vaulting political fault lines . . . it was evident that for most of the participants, the multilaterals were seen as a 'win/win' situation."[14] These talks are open to regional and extra-regional parties.

Notwithstanding the absence of Syria and Lebanon, which have refused to participate until there is progress in the bilateral negotiations, the multilaterals have served the concrete benefit of continuing even in the face of events on the ground that have disrupted the bilaterals. Thus, even while bilateral negotiations have been postponed and suspended due to events in the region, the multilaterals talks have continued—as have the "inter-sessionals," activities involving members of the various parties, including preparatory workshops, visits to research centers, and trips to observe confidence-building measures in Europe.[15] They have served as a forum in which the various parties can express their concerns, float ideas, and gauge reactions without any form of commitment. For the participants, they have served the important function of familiarization with each other's "goals and intentions . . . perceptions and anxieties . . . [and] flexibility and limits,"[16] as well as methods of surmounting problems and identifying the benefits of cooperative action. They are thus central to the Madrid peace process, the goal of which is to "begin to break down the mutual suspicions and mistrust that perpetuate the conflict."[17]

Within each of the multilaterals the topics are further broken down; for example, the potential of linking communication and transportation networks are among the topics being examined by the working group on economic development.[18] One advantage of dealing with issues narrowly defined and bringing together experts from regional and extra-regional parties is that opinions, fears, concerns, and alternative solutions are raised and, hopefully, some consensus can develop. That is, an "epistemic community," defined as "a network of professionals with recognized expertise and competence in a particular domain and an authoritative claim to policy-relevant knowledge within that domain or issue-area,"[19] might develop and affect decisions at the policy-making level. Indeed, former Assistant Secretary of State Edward Djerejian pointed out this goal when he noted that in each of the multilaterals there has been a need to learn the basics, identify problems, and obtain information. Concerning the multilateral working group on the environment he observed that:

The mode of operation has been to bring experts—not politicians or diplomats—from the region together at workshops. . . .What we found was that when we put these experts together they solved problems. Beyond the glare of the political klieg lights, we created an environment where scientists spoke the same language.[20]

Another goal of the multilateral talks has been to "demonstrate that peace will bring concrete benefits to all of the peoples of the region."[21] Among the most important benefits of cooperation is an improvement in the region's economic situation. Given the considerable ambivalence, and the existence of embedded opposition toward the peace process among the populaces of the parties involved,[22] there is a need to make clear not only the real costs of continued conflict but also the substantial gains to be made through peace. As former U.S. Secretary of State Baker noted:

Parties in the process cannot reasonably be expected to operate outside their political environment; but they should be expected to educate, shape, and lead politics and opinion.[23]

One of the methods of increasing knowledge of and interest in the benefits of the multilateral talks is provided through what is traditionally called "track-two" diplomacy,[24] but in this case might be called "track-three." That is, through meetings among officials, academics, policy experts, and concerned individuals in non-official forums, the free exchange of views can be encouraged, trial-balloons launched, and personal relations developed. The benefits of such efforts include widening support for the process, introducing perspectives that might not otherwise receive attention, and facilitating feedback into the official process.

THE IMPORTANCE OF PRACTICAL PEACEMAKING

This volume and its companion[25] are the outcome of one such non-official effort. Growing out of a conference addressing the five multilateral talks—water, the environment, refugees, economic cooperation and development, and arms control and regional security—and jointly sponsored by the Institute on Global Conflict and Cooperation and the Center for International Relations of the University of California in June, 1993, this conference brought together North American and Middle Eastern scholars and researchers—including, in a non-official capacity, participants in the official peace process—to discuss the problems facing the regional actors and methods of addressing them. This combination of participants was intended to ensure an open exchange of ideas and to mix speculation that could provide guidance for the future with practical experience. Indeed, some of the more visionary chapters are by participants who are directly engaged in the official process. This volume reflects that conference and, because of the inclusion of participants in the peace process, it provides a "snapshot" in time of issues raised in the multilateral talks on arms control and regional security.

The book examines the possible role for a variety of actions, whether verbal or concrete, that can be taken by Israel and the Arabs to demonstrate their interest in peace and then, once peace is achieved, to reinforce agreements. The emphasis is on steps that are *practical*, in that they both draw on previous experience and can actually be used in practice. Indeed, the three principles derived from the Egyptian–Israeli experience—gradualism, direct contacts, and practical steps—implicitly form the bases of the analyses and suggestions. Some suggestions may strike the reader as idealistic, unrealistic, or impractical. While there would be good reason for such an impression, we can only note that the suggestion that Israel and the Palestine Liberation Organization should, much less would, recognize each other, enter into bilateral negotiations, and then begin a process of devolution of authority in the Occupied Territories would have seemed incredulous until it actually happened. The suggestions made by the contributors in this volume are based on a realistic analysis of what is possible given current conditions, what is necessary to move the peace process forward and solidify future peace agreements, and the interconnection between the two.

The emphasis in the initial section is on broad goals and specific proposals that can both facilitate the peace process and strengthen agreements when they are reached. The second section raises some of the concerns and impediments that could impede progress unless they are either addressed or there is at least tacit agreement to put them aside. The third section deals with verification. The success of any agreement will depend largely on the confidence of its signatories that its terms are being met, and in turn that confidence will be influenced by verification measures. As former President Reagan put it, "Trust, but verify." The final section of the book examines the crucial role of politics in Arab–Israeli relations and explores the possible role of an institutional structure to sustain the peace process and strengthen peace.

THE NATURE OF ARMS CONTROL AND REGIONAL SECURITY

While arms control and regional security are intimately linked, that the scope of each is different is apparent in the following chapters. The domain of arms control is limited to military issues. Regional security is a broader concept, encompassing not only the military but also economics and politics—that is, anything that can pose a threat to the security of any of the regional parties and thus, given the geographic size of the region and the linkages among the actors, to the region as a whole. To an extent this difference in emphasis is based on differing perspectives of the causes of conflict and methods of ameliorating it. For example, if conflict, or more specifically warfare, is caused by military instability arising from arms races, changes in the balance of power, and vulnerabilities whether perceived or real, then the solution lies in developing an arms control regime that creates greater certainty and stability. On the other hand, if regional conflict is caused by political and economic insecurities, then addressing these problems will enhance regional stability.

To a certain extent this distinction is artificial. As Israeli Foreign Minister Shimon Peres argues in his recent book, appropriately entitled *The New Middle East*, there are direct links between the conflict, high levels of military spending, and the economic problems confronting the Middle East.[26] As Ahmed Fakhr notes in his contribution to this volume, arms control and peace agreements hold potential economic benefits by reducing military spending. The increased stability generated by such agreements will allow the regional states to concentrate on their economies and also make the region more attractive to outside investment and, not incidentally, tourism.

The extent of convergence among the contributors to this volume, among different nationalities and between scholars and practitioners, is most impressive. In broad outline they speak the same "language," define the issues similarly, and frequently make similar recommendations. Among the central identified goals for arms control are the need to enhance stability to minimize the risks of accidental war, to provide reassurance concerning intentions, and to positively affect the psychological environment, including public opinion. under the broad rubric of confidence-building measures (CBMs), a panoply of steps to enhance stability is suggested.

There is also agreement on the means, specifically the need for gradualism, or what Michael Intriligator refers to as the strategy of Graduated and Reciprocated Reduction in Tensions (GRIT). This step-by-step approach applies to the types of CBMs that are appropriate at different stages of the peace process and, relatedly, the effect they have on military capabilities. The initial step would consist of the renunciation of the threat or use of force, which would have political and psychological effects but would not affect military capabilities. As Abdullah Toukan argues, however, such a declaration would have implications for additional steps, including those that affect military capabilities, that could be taken during the interim and final stages of the peace process.

As both Mark Heller and M.Z. Diab point out, strengthening deterrence is a condition for and goal of arms control, but this considerably complicates any design of an arms control regime. As deterrence is based on making the costs of any war outweigh its possible benefits, the military forces required for deterrence are frequently indistinguishable from those useful for an attack. The large number of possible CBMs is thus beneficial, as it provides a varied menu from which choices and tradeoffs are possible. The need for tradeoffs is particularly important given, as both Diab and Gerald Steinberg emphasize, the various asymmetries—in terms of population, territory, size and role of the military, and technological capabilities—between Israel and the Arabs. The territorial asymmetry is likely to increase if, as Diab argues, a requirement for peace and an arms control regime is eventual Israeli withdrawal from lands occupied in the 1967 war, which will, in turn, require Israel, according to Steinberg, to maintain its nuclear deterrent. There is a potential for a tradeoff here, one implicitly recognized by most of the contributors, who suggest that grappling with the contentious issue of nuclear, chemical, and biological weapons should be left until after a period of peace has been sustained. That is, as these issues are particularly contentious, they may impede the peace process if introduced prematurely.

During the period in which peace is being built, as both Toukan and Heller point out, a key function of CBMs is to provide tests by which each party can gauge the intentions of the others. This function becomes both more important and more difficult as the process moves from declaratory CBMs to those that have concrete effects on the militaries of the various countries. A breach of a commitment that is not discovered or is discovered belatedly can lead to war, whether accidental or deliberate, while the suspicion that a commitment has been broken can lead to distrust and undermine the peace process. Therefore, implementation and verification are critical issues in the design of any arms control and security regime. In turn, knowledge of the technologies available for verifying compliance with an arms control agreement can facilitate it, while concerns identified by negotiators can guide experts in their development of technologies. There is a need, Arian Pregenzer and John Taylor argue, for increased interaction between the technical and political communities. Lawrence Scheinman looks forward to the possible implementation of a Middle East Nuclear Weapon Free Zone and identifies its possible guidelines and methods of implementation; as he notes, this issue is of global and not only regional concern.

The ability of the regional states to progress toward peace and then sustain agreements reached is largely dependent upon their political situations. Etel Solingen identifies how domestic coalitions influence the policies of regional states and argues that the gradualism of the peace process helps acclimate public opinion and, when combined with direct evidence of the benefits of peace, helps strengthen the position of those favoring liberalization and, consequently, peace. Should the severe economic, social, and political problems not be addressed, warns Yezid Sayigh, various regional states face potential collapse. Domestic instability has the potential to spread, whether via inter-state conflict or through destabilization of the politics of other states. Conversely, domestic stability increases the chances for regional stability.

The goals of the peace process, of which the multilateral talks on arms control and regional security are a part, are complex and multifaceted. Stability, economic development, justice, and the improvement of the lives of the region's inhabitants are interlinked. The chances of achieving these goals will be improved, according to a number of contributors, if both the process and the eventual peace are institutionalized. Institutions, whether regional or global, can play an important role in verification of arms control agreements and a potential nuclear-weapon-free zone. More ambitiously, argue Toukan and Sayigh, a permanent institutionalization process, along the lines of the Conference of Security and Cooperation in Europe (CSCE), can provide a valuable forum for the discussion of issues before they become conflicts. Such routinized meetings, exchange of views, recognition of interdependency and communal problems, identification of possible tradeoffs and joint solutions, and mutual familiarization can play an important role in stabilizing expectations and, over time, transforming narrow conceptions of security based on the nation and state, to the broader concept emphasized by a number of contributors—and regional security.

PROGRESS IN THE PEACE PROCESS

Since the conference from which this volume grew was held in June 1993, dramatic progress has been made in the peace process. Some of the recommendations made by the contributors to this volume have been implemented. Prior to signing the Declaration of Principles (DOP), Israel and the PLO exchanged letters of mutual recognition and the latter renounced terrorism and violence.[27] The DOP itself laid out a timeline for the transferring of responsibility for a variety of issues from Israel to the Palestinian authorities with an interim period in which each side can test the intentions of the other and build support for additional steps. It also included a commitment to negotiate the final status of the Occupied Territories on the basis of United Nations Resolutions 242 and 338. Similarly, the 1994 Israel–Jordan breakthrough Declaration, which preceeded their peace treaty, included mutual recognition of the "sovereignty, territorial integrity and political independence of every state in the area" and a pledge to "avoid threats and the use of force."[28] The Declaration also included a number of CBMs, including cooperation between the Israel and Jordanian police forces to combat crime and smuggling (cf. Heller), the linking of electricity grids "as part of a regional concept," and opening border crossings for tourists.[29]

CONCLUSION

The multilaterals provide a context for considering the future payoffs of the Middle East peace process—the benefits of a situation in which all might cooperate in the future, or at least a situation in which the level of acrimony is reduced. For the first time ever, Arabs and Israelis are together seeking to develop a vision of a common future. In this sense, if the bilaterals attempt to reduce the problems of the past, the multilaterals are, at least in part, detailing the promise of a better region in the future.

The Arms Control and Regional Security (ACRS) talks in particular hold the key to creating a region in which the fear of catastrophic conflict can be reduced along the road to prosperity. These talks can help prevent conflict by reducing misunderstandings, developing confidence- and security-building measures, eventually leading to arms control and reduction, and changes in force structures and doctrines. These issues are central to peace and stability in the Middle East, and they are the focus of the multilateral talks on arms control and regional security. It is therefore to these particular talks that we now turn in the following essays.

NOTES

1. An important report on these forums is the *Bulletin of Regional Cooperation in the Middle East* (Washington, DC: Search for Common Ground).

2. See Yaacov Bar-Siman-Tov, "The Arab–Israeli Conflict: Learning Conflict Resolution," *Journal of Peace Research*, 31 (1994).

3. Brian Mandell, "Anatomy of a Confidence-Building Regime: Egyptian–Israeli Security Cooperation, 1973–1979," *International Journal*, 45 (Spring, 1990).

4. Text in William Quandt, *The Peace Process* (Washington: The Brookings Institution, 1993), p. 467.

5. John Hannah, *At Arms Length: Soviet–Syrian Relations in the Gorbachev Era*. Policy Paper No. 18. (Washington, D.C.: Washington Institute for Near East Policy, 1988).

6. See Steven L. Spiegel, "The United States and the Middle East," in Ami Ayalon, ed., *Middle East Contemporary Survey* (Boulder: Westview Press, 1990) and Steven L. Spiegel and David J. Pervin, "The United States and the Middle East," in Ami Ayalon, ed., *Middle East Contemporary Survey* (Boulder: Westview Press, 1991).

7. See Richard Bulliet, "The Future of the Islamic Movement," *Foreign Affairs*, 72:5 (November/December, 1993).

8. See Janice Gross Stein, "The Alchemy of Peacemaking: The Prerequisites and Corequisites of Progress in the Arab–Israeli Conflict," *International Journal* 38:4 (Autumn, 1983) 531–555, especially 553.

9. On the rationales behind the longstanding Arab and Israeli conditions, see Saadia Touval, "Frameworks for Arab–Israeli Negotiations—What Difference Do They Make?" *Negotiation Journal*, 3:1 (January, 1987) 37–52.

10. Secretary of State James Baker, "Opening Remarks at the Middle East Peace Conference," Madrid, November 1, 1991, *United States Department of State Dispatch* 3:Supplement 2 (February, 1992), 11.

11. On the strengths and weaknesses of multilateral negotiations, see Saadia Touval, "Multilateral Negotiation: An Analytical Approach," *Negotiation Journal*, 5:2 (April, 1989).

12. For a similar argument, see Alfred Leroy Atherton, Jr., "The Shifting Sands of Middle East Peace," *Foreign Policy* 86 (Spring, 1992), 124.

13. Secretary of State James Baker, "Concluding Remarks," Organizational Meeting for Multilateral Negotiations on the Middle East, Moscow, January 28, 1992, *United States Department of State Dispatch* 3: Supplement 2 (February, 1992), 27.

14. Assistant Secretary of State Edward Djerejian, "The Multilateral Talks in the Arab–Israeli Peace Process," Speech to the Washington Institute for Near East Policy, September 22, 1993.

15. Joel Peters, *Building Bridges: The Arab–Israeli Multilateral Talks* (London: Royal Institute of International Affairs, 1994).

16. Ibid., p. 34.

17. "U.S. Soviet Invitation to the Mideast Peace Conference in Madrid, October 18, 1991," in Quandt, 503.

18. Peters, op. cit., 29.

19. See Peter M. Haas, "Introduction: Epistemic Communities and International Policy Coordination," *International Organization*, 48:1 (Winter, 1992), 1–36, at 3.

20. Assistant Secretary of State Djerejian, op. cit.

21. Assistant Secretary of State Edward Djerejian, Statement before the Subcommittee on Europe and the Middle East, House Foreign Affairs Committee, July 27, 1993, 4.

22. For example, see Hilal Khashan, "Are the Arabs Ready for Peace with Israel?" *Middle East Quarterly*, 1:1 (March, 1994), 19–28, and Asher Arian, *Israeli Security and the Peace Process: Public Opinion in 1994* (Tel Aviv: Jaffee Center for Strategic Studies Memorandum No. 43, 1994).

23. Secretary of State Baker, "Opening Remarks," Madrid, November 1, 1991, op. cit., 11.

24. On track-two diplomacy, see Joseph Montville, "The Arrow and the Olive Branch: A Case for Track Two Diplomacy," in John McDonald and Diane Bendahmane, eds., *Conflict Resolution: Track Two Diplomacy* (Washington, DC: Foreign Service Institute, 1987).

25. Steven L. Spiegel and David J. Pervin, eds., *Practical Peacemaking in the Middle East, Vol. II: The Environment, Water, Refugees and Economic Cooperation and Development* (New York: Garland Publishing, forthcoming).

26. Shimon Peres, *The New Middle East* (New York: Henry Holt, 1993).

27. *New York Times*, September 10, 1993.

28. *New York Times*, July 26, 1994.

29. Ibid.

The Goals of Arms Control and
Regional Security

2   The Middle East Peace Process, Arms Control, and Regional Security

Abdullah Toukan

INTRODUCTION

Over the past four decades there have been a number of arms control initiatives and proposals for the Middle East, from the early 1950s Tripartite (U.S., France, and U.K.) Agreement to limit arms in the region, through the 1974 Nuclear Weapon Free Zone (NWFZ) proposal put forward to the U.N. General Assembly by Egypt and co-sponsored by Iran, culminating with the 1991 U.S. arms control initiatives.[1] All failed. Yet notwithstanding the disappointments of the past, the Middle East peace process initiated at Madrid should provide an opportunity for achieving the objective of establishing a broad security framework structure for the various steps and measures toward arms control in the region.

THE MIDDLE EAST PEACE PROCESS

The present Middle East peace negotiations are conducted in two parallel forums: bilateral and multilateral. The bilateral negotiations are being conducted in four independent tracks:

Palestinian–Israeli, Syria–Israeli, Lebanon–Israeli, and Jordan–Israeli. The basis of the negotiations, outlined in the letters of invitation to the Madrid Middle East Peace Conference,[2] is United Nations Security Council Resolutions (UNSCRs) 242 and 338. The Lebanese invitation was based on United Nations Resolutions 425 and 426, regarding southern Lebanon. The final outcome of the negotiations would be a comprehensive, just, and lasting peace. The center stage is the Palestinian–Israeli track. The framework of this track, as outlined in the Declarations of Principles signed on September 13, 1993, consists of an Interim/Transitional period of five years during which the Palestinian self-government authority will be established in the West Bank and Gaza. Before the beginning of the third year of this phase, negotiations will start on the final status of these territories for the purpose of implementating UNSCRs 242 and 338.

The first organizational meeting for the Multilateral Middle East peace negotiations took place in Moscow on January 1992. The U.S. Secretary of State, James Baker III, set the initial guidelines for the working groups:[3]

> What we are embarking upon here in Moscow is in no way a substitute for what we are trying to promote in the bilateral negotiations. Only the bilateral talks can address and one day resolve the basic issues of territory, security and peace which the parties have identified as the core elements of a lasting comprehensive peace between Israel and its Arab neighbors. . . . In short, the multilateral talks are intended as a complement to the bilateral negotiations; each can and will buttress the other.

After the organizational meeting, Secretary Baker explained the potential for the multilateral talks:

> •   We should not forget the potential for the multilateral talks to help create a political environment in which the

bilateral talks are more likely to accomplish what we all want in the areas of peace, territory and security.

•   We should take full advantage of the experience, the expertise and resources of others, both inside and outside the region.

•   While keeping our horizons and ambitions broad, it might be best if we were to focus initially on some small, practical steps that provide a foundation on which we can build.[4]

Consequently, five working groups were formed: *Water* chaired by the U.S.; *Environment* chaired by Japan; *Economic Development* chaired by the European union; *Refugees* chaired by Canada; and *Arms Control and Regional Security* co-chaired by the U.S. and Russia. Each working group consists of regional and extra-regional parties.

Given the two frameworks of bilateral and multilateral talks, the critical issue is how to integrate them within a defined time-frame of reference. The time-frame established by the Israeli–Palestinian Declaration of Principles may serve as a model. The Palestinian–Israeli negotiations started with the negotiation phase, will moved to a transitional/interim period, and will conclude with an agreement on the final status. Within each of these phases there will be intermediate stages, each with its own objective. At each stage the multilaterals may make a contribution.

A second question revolves around how to simultaneously integrate the regional security dimension into the political process from the start, leading eventually to a regional cooperative security framework. Such a framework should be thought of in the broadest sense of the definition of security, incorporating economic, political, military and humanitarian dimensions. Two final questions are how to carry the peace process forward into the long term and how to sustain, maintain, and guarantee all the peace treaties and agreements reached in the bilateral and multilateral negotiations.

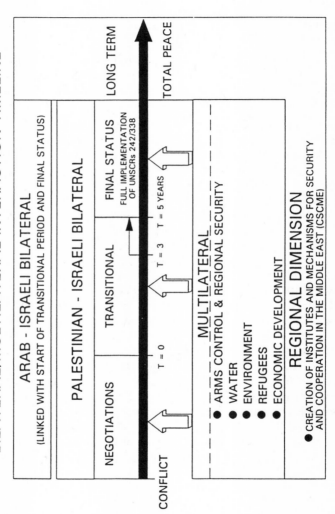

Toukan, Figure 1: Bilateral–Multilateral Interaction Timeline

ARMS CONTROL

Arms control can be considered as any measure that reduces the likelihood of war as an instrument of policy or that limits the destructiveness and duration of war should it break out. It is not only technical, meaning arms reductions or disarmament, but also has a political nature, encompassing any measure that strengthens regional security and diminishes the utility of military force as an instrument of national policy.

Arms control can be categorized as "structural" and "operational."[5] Structural arms control aims at limiting or reducing manpower and military equipment—conventional and non-conventional—ultimately producing agreements to make major reductions in forces. Operational arms control involves efforts, such as those carried out in the context of the Conference on Security and Cooperation in Europe (CSCE), to implement confidence- and security-building measures (CSBMs). CSBMs have one main objective: to provide transparency and thereby predictability, thus serving to prevent a surprise attack and to ensure that the forces of one's potential adversary are not of an offensive character. CSBMs can be divided into two levels; technical military CSBMs, at the operational level of military policy, and political-military CSBMs, declarations of intent concerning the planned use of forces and/or weapons. For example, the renunciation of the first use of force makes it possible to contemplate changes in the order of battle, force structure posture, and military doctrines. Hence we can say that CSBMs are arrangements designed to enhance confidence and address security concerns at both levels of operations: military planning and national security policy.

We should point out that there are other CSBMs, universal in nature, such as humanitarian, economic, and diplomatic measures. These can be considered as peace process gestures and measures that could give support to the negotiations. At times these have a greater impact in altering the political climate of the negotiations than in directly affecting the military capabilities of the parties involved. Yet, as noted above, they are central to a broad conception of security.

REGIONAL SECURITY DIMENSIONS

The geographic definition of the region should be kept flexible. The present regional parties attending the multilateral negotiations can certainly be considered as a group of states with political, security and economic links that can initially define the region. Once general and reciprocal declaratory principles are reached, followed by the generation and implementation of region specific arms control measures, they subsequently can be enhanced to encourage other states to join. If stability can be achieved in the region by promoting arms control measures, this will have a positive effect on other regions. For this very reason security concerns of peripheral states as well as other regions should be taken into consideration throughout the process. Ultimately, the geographical boundaries of the region and sub-regions will have to be defined.

THE POLITICAL FRAMEWORK FOR CSBMS

In this section the experience of two regions in which CSBMs have been extensively applied is reviewed. While the technologies employed to carry out these measures may be very similar in all regions, the content of messages and information exchanged are certainly different in each case. As part of the ongoing Middle East peace negotiations, it could be beneficial and certainly educational for states within the region to visit and study the technical structures and modes of operation of some of these centers, such as those in Europe. Such knowledge of how technical CSBMs have been implemented in other regions, combined with the political-military guiding principles based on

UNSCR 242, can be the basis of studies of certain CSBMs—including types, scope and applicability—generated for the region, to be applied at the appropriate time as reinforcement of and support for the bilateral negotiations.

The Middle East has experience with CSBMs, most notably in the Sinai.[6] Yet the dynamic between the current Arab–Israeli peace negotiations and the implementation of CSBMs is the complete reverse from that which characterized the Egyptian–Israeli peace process that begin soon after the 1973 War. In other words, military CSBMs should be an outcome of the present peace talks rather than an Arab–Israeli peace accord as an outcome of military CSBMs, as was the case between Israel and Egypt.

After the October 1973 war, several agreements were signed between Israel and Syria and between Egypt and Israel. All these agreements included military aspects relating to the separation of forces as well as to restrictions on the amount of forces and equipment in specific territorial zones. Accordingly, they also included verification regimes and control measures to ensure both their execution and long-term maintenance.

The Israel–Syria Separation of Forces Agreement (31 May 1974) was signed within the framework of the Geneva Conference, with the participation of the U.S. and Soviet representatives as co-chairmen. The agreement included lines of separation between forces, limitations of manpower, weapons systems deployed behind the lines of separation, and verification and control measures to be executed by the U.N. peacekeeping force.

The Israeli–Egyptian Separation of Forces Agreement was signed on 18 January 1974, at the 101st kilometer of the Suez Cairo road, by the chiefs of staff of both nations. The U.S. became a guarantor of the agreements; it was also involved in operating verification regimes in the various agreements between Israel and Egypt.

The Israeli–Egyptian Interim Agreement was signed on 4 September 1975. Its main elements included provisions for the redeployment of forces (Israeli forces moved eastward in Sinai); the establishment of a buffer zone between the forces where a United Nations Emergency Force (UNEF) was deployed; for the limited deployment of forces and weapons systems in the zones adjacent to the buffer zone; and for a comprehensive verification regime constructed to monitor its execution. The UNEF established a complex network of verification means. For its part, the United States operated the U.S. Sinai Support Mission. Israel and Egypt alike operated early warning stations and had liaison staffs.

The conclusion reached by a number of analysts is that the prompt execution of the Interim Agreement and the successful operation of its complex verification regime created the atmosphere and confidence needed for completion of the Israeli–Egyptian Peace Accord in 1979. The Camp David Accords were signed on 17 September 1978, and the Peace Agreement between Israel and Egypt took place on 26 March 1979.

As the current peace negotiations are based on letters of invitation and assurances that the whole peace process would be based on United Nations Security Council Resolutions 242 and 338 (on the principle of land for peace), the final goal was essentially stated and defined from the beginning. In contrast to the Egyptian–Israeli experience, it is not a process in which Jordan, Syria, Lebanon, the Palestinians, and Israel sit together and try to reach some common goal, necessitating CSBMs that could help the respective parties in achieving some form of peace accord. The goal was clearly defined and is based on a political solution, and the modalities to achieve the goal of a just, lasting, and comprehensive peace based on UNSCRs 242 and 338 are presently being worked on. After a political solution is reached and the process moves into the implementation phase, security arrangements and verification and monitoring on the agreed upon borders could take place, coupled with CSBMs in both the bilateral and multilateral settings.

There is also extensive experience with military CSBMs in Europe.[7] Yet while it has been suggested that Middle Eastern parties might learn about the modalities and capabilities, especially technical, of European CSBMs, it is important to keep in mind the fundamentally different political circumstances that distinguish the two regions. In Europe there have been no major conflicts or wars since 1949, and a general consensus existed on the geographical boundaries of the region and the territorial borders of states within the region. There was also consensus on the illegitimacy of the use of military force—especially as a means of changing borders among states. In Europe the approach to security is less dependent on military strategies or arms procurement and more linked to political and economic cooperation. In Europe an institutional infrastructure—made up of the CSCE, European Union, and NATO—gives the various parties confidence in bilateral and multilateral agreements and treaties.

In the Middle East, in contrast, there have been six wars between Israel and the Arabs, conflict among the Arab states, and two wars in the Gulf. The Middle East region is ill defined geographically, extending, according to some, from Morocco to Pakistan. Nor is there consensus on borders; indeed the Arab–Israeli peace negotiations are based upon Israel withdrawing from land it is presently occupying. In some parts of the Middle East, military force is still considered as an acceptable means of changing territorial borders and as an instrument for achieving policy goals. Most countries in the region believe that military strength will deter military aggression; thus they will not accept any form of arms control until regional peace is established.

ARMS CONTROL MEASURES AND THE MIDDLE EAST PEACE PROCESS

The connection between the multilateral talks on arms control and regional security and the bilateral negotiations can be thought of as two tracks of a railroad, running parallel and connected by many ties. In the negotiations phase the parties should present their "National Views on Long Term Objectives on Arms Control and Regional Security," as was done in the multilateral Arms Control and Regional Security (ACRS) working group. This will help clarify intentions and provide a clearer understanding of security concerns and threat perceptions. Combined with declaratory statements, basic guiding principles—an example being the Helsinki Final Act Declaration of Principles—can be drawn up and can become the common political basis upon which the multilateral working groups can work. Such principles can establish codes of conduct (rules of the road). Subsequently, region specific arms control measures (operational and structural) can then be generated.

The initial group of principles could be directly extrapolated from UNSCR 242. Such declaratory principles could include:

- acknowledgment of the inadmissibility of the acquisition of territory by war;

- respect for and acknowledgment of the sovereignty, territorial integrity and political independence of every state in the region;

- recognition of the rights of all to live in peace within secure and recognized boundaries free from threats or acts of war;

- equal rights and self-determination of peoples;

- the need to settle disputes by peaceful means;

- non-intervention in the internal affairs of states.

We can then add to these fundamental principles a number of arms control declaratory principles and appropriate measures at each phase of the bilateral negotiations. In order to reduce the risks of war and increase the likelihood of a sustained peace, CSBMs must be significant in scope and politically as well as legally binding. Since the primary objective of CSBMs is to reduce the risks of armed conflict among states, they will play a crucial role during the transition from war or conflict to total peace.

Let us consider for instance the principle of "refraining from the threat or use of force," either in furthering policy goals or changing territorial boundaries. Translating this into a practical and applicable action will require "transparency" and "openness." This in turn implies the exchange of information on military activities, including military exercises and movement of troops.

Reflecting back on the Palestinian–Israeli bilateral negotiations time-line, what better time than the transitional period, when the withdrawal of Israeli troops from the West Bank, Gaza, and other Arab occupied territories takes place, should parties start applying technical-military CSBMs in order to lower tensions and the likelihood of misunderstanding, thereby reducing the suspicions of any surprise attacks? Declaratory principles can also start generating structural arms control measures. In order to reduce tensions, there could be a freeze or partial change in military structures as well as control of buildup of the military in terms of certain offensive weapon systems. Furthermore, declaratory principles that address the proliferation of weapons of mass destruction and the need to establish a weapons of mass destruction free zone will certainly generate technical-military CSBMs as well as structural arms control measures. These could include a freeze on the acquisition and production of and any relevant research and development on weapons of mass destruction material, such as uranium, separated plutonium and other elements used in nuclear weapons manufacture. There could also be a freeze on, and eventual elimination of, delivery systems such as ballistic missiles. In essence there will be a one-to-one mapping between the political-military declaratory principles and the related technical-military CSBMs, verification and monitoring, and structural arms control measures.

The present Middle East peace process basically provides us with a broad structural framework for integrating CSBMs in the various phases of the process: the negotiations phase, the transitional/interim period, and the final status and long term. During the bilateral negotiations phase, in which security as well as political and economic arrangements are being agreed upon and drawn up, the multilateral ACRS process can start generating declaratory principles which should be politically and legally binding and can generate arms control measures. In addition, the parties at this stage can start taking advantage of the experience of extra-regional countries with arms control. Finally, it is important that all past arms control proposals should be studied and re-evaluated at this stage.

Once the transitional phase of the bilateral negotiations begin—we can consider this milestone to be time zero—initial applications of appropriate technical-military as well as structural arms control could start. Regional parties can continue with declaratory principles, for this will signal readiness to make legally binding obligations in addition to politically binding commitments. Eventually, when the transitional phase moves into the final status in the bilateral negotiations, full implementation of technical and structural arms control measures can take place. The full implementation stage can continue into the long-term, post-peace treaty. Here again declaratory principles can continue to be explored as new political and strategic developments occur in the region. A word of caution is appropriate at this point, in that if a declaration of principle is made and the behavior of parties is inconsistent or even contrary to the principles, then this will undermine the

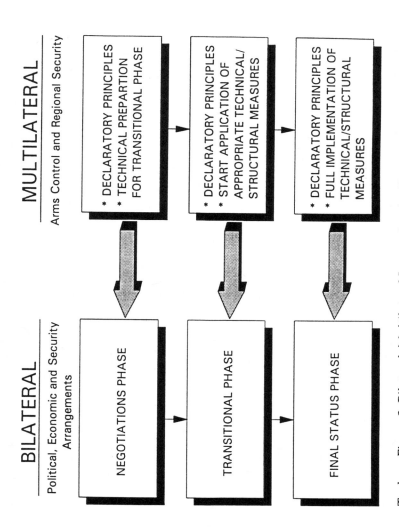

MULTILATERAL

Arms Control and Regional Security

* DECLARATORY PRINCIPLES
* TECHNICAL PREPARTION FOR TRANSITIONAL PHASE

* DECLARATORY PRINCIPLES
* START APPLICATION OF APPROPRIATE TECHNICAL/ STRUCTURAL MEASURES

* DECLARATORY PRINCIPLES
* FULL IMPLEMENTATION OF TECHNICAL/STRUCTURAL MEASURES

BILATERAL

Political, Economic and Security Arrangements

NEGOTIATIONS PHASE

TRANSITIONAL PHASE

FINAL STATUS PHASE

Toukan, Figure 2: Bilateral–Multilateral Interaction, by Negotiations Phase process and even have a negative effect on confidence-building in general in the region.

During the bilateral negotiations, the primary objective of the parties is to begin CSBMs that increase each party's confidence that its national security will be preserved and even enhanced after the peace settlement is reached. Initially there could be a series of political-military CSBMs during negotiations, in the form of declarations of intent. Among the issues that could be addressed are:

- the need to address the dangers of an uncontrolled arms race;

- the proliferation of weapons of mass destruction;

- the non-use of aggression or force to achieve political aims;

- the need to control arms transfers to the region;

- the need to regulate arms production in the region;

- the urgency to sign the NPT treaty and accept IAEA safeguards, to demonstrate compliance with agreed standards of behavior;

- the need to address the establishment of a Weapons of Mass Destruction Free Zone (WMDFZ) covering nuclear, biological, and chemical weapons;

- the need to address the proliferation of ballistic missiles;

- the need to create and strengthen regional institutions such as a conflict prevention /resolution center and an inter-regional verification and monitoring agency.

Coupled to the above there should be a number of CSBMs that can be applied within the bilateral negotiations.

During the transitional period, there will be a gradual phasing in and implementation of a political and security regime in the West Bank and Gaza as well as the start of Israeli troop withdrawal from Syrian, Lebanese, and Jordanian territories. Arms control measures (operational and structural) in this phase could include CSBMs that are political-military and technical-military in nature, such as:

- applying verification and monitoring means on borders;

- applying appropriate CSBMs when and if necessary to support and reinforce bilateral and multilateral agreements (here we can consider some CSCE-type of CSBMs);

- starting a partial change to military structures;

- initiating a freeze on military build-up and arms procurement;

- beginning an official register of all arms transfers to the region;

- banning the re-export of certain types of weapons;

- starting discussions on the quality and quantity of the acquisition of certain types of weapons;

- beginning a freeze on the acquisition, production and testing of ballistic missiles by Middle East countries;

- initiating a ban on the production, acquisition, and any relevant research on enriched uranium, separated plutonium, and other elements used in nuclear weapons;

- introducing verification and monitoring measures concerning chemical and biological weapons in the region;

- creating institutions for a Weapons of Mass Destruction Free Zone.

In the final status, long-term arrangements in structural and operational arms control could include:

- full on-site monitoring and verification (conventional and non-conventional arms);

- a reduction in forces;

- establishment of a regional agency to regulate arms transfers, with official information on weapons procurement;

- regulation of domestic arms production;

- initial implementation of a WMDFZ in the region;

- work toward the elimination of ballistic missiles;

- establishment of a fully active conflict prevention/ resolution center;

- establishment of a fully active inter-regional verification institute;

- drafting of regional and sub-regional CSBMs;

- expansion of regional security framework.

VERIFICATION AND MONITORING

Verification and monitoring agreements are essential for successful arms control. They deal with gathering, processing/collating, and disseminating information from national or (international) technical means in order to assess parties' compliance with arms control agreements' provisions regarding military activities and structural limitations. Any verification agreement will necessarily have to address all sides' concerns along three dimensions:

1. the required level of confidence that all sides are adhering to the provisions. The confidence level can range from absolute, to adequate, to limited, to token.

2. the types and degree of intrusiveness of verification methods. There are different levels of inspection and detection methodologies, ranging from general routine inspections, selective on-site inspection, on-site challenge inspection, national/international technical means, and CSBMs.

3. the types of verification systems, including existing and projected national and international technical means. Among the types of monitoring methods are overhead flights, photo reconnaissance satellites, remote sensing, seismic sensors, and electronic intelligence. There are also a number of technologies for synthesizing, analyzing, and disseminating information gained from monitoring.

DECLARATORY PRINCIPLES AND THE PROLIFERATION OF BALLISTIC MISSILES

The proliferation of ballistic missiles and the transfer of technologies associated with their production have been a great concern to the world community. A number of regimes have been established, such as the Missile Technology Control Regime (MTCR), as well as arms control initiatives for a freeze and ultimate elimination of these missiles in the region. In this section we show how a politically binding declaratory statement—consequently becoming legally binding—can generate technical-military CSBMs and various verification measures.

Suppose we start with the declaratory statement that "we need to address the proliferation of ballistic missiles." Now the typical life-cycle of a weapon system undergoes the following stages:[8]

- research and development;
- testing;
- production;
- deployment;
- storage;
- transfer (internally, internationally, export);
- withdrawal and destruction.

Each stage has its own set of observable areas of activity amenable to verification, depending on the level of confidence required. If we consider the political and legal commitment for the freeze on the production of surface-to-surface missiles, a typical set of observable areas for production verification could include the following:[9]

- the nature and quantity of inputs introduced into the production facility, (such as strap down inertial navigation systems, composite material, liquid or solid propellant fuel elements);
- building/facilities configurations, including special safety equipment;
- associated facilities (testing, ranges, wastes);
- number and types of employees;
- outputs (transport launchers, storage of products).

These observable areas of activity will be subject to a verification methodology and system of monitoring. However, all on-site verification techniques as well as overhead flights definitely have to come after a full peace treaty goes into effect. On the other hand, certain CSBMs, as part of the verification agreement, can play a major role in paving the way for the future comprehensive verification and monitoring. CSBMs can be applied while the regional states are striving toward the final stages of a peace treaty, not only in the negotiations phase. Typically these CSBMs could be of military-industrial production transparency, and may include: exchange of military industrial plans and information, publications of military budgets, exchange of scientific publications, military to military contacts through third parties (in the initial stages), seminars, and conferences.

Finally, if it is at the "testing" stage that we are interested in verifying compliance, then the potential observable activities that apply to production may also apply to testing. Other areas would include:[10]

- destructive effects (e.g., craters, environmental);
- telemetry;
- field organization for the test;
- specialized facilities (e.g., launch sites).

Again, certain CSBMs, such as test pre-notification or on-site visits to test facilities can play a major role in verification. However, CSBMs that are not based upon a political obligation that is also legally binding, can end up as symbolic in nature and potentially ignored at any time. Such a breach of a political obligation would in effect cause more damage than if it was never applied. Hence, for technical-military CSBMs to be applied effectively in type and scope, they require a political and legal framework that is binding.

COOPERATIVE SECURITY AND THE CSCME PROCESS

We start this section by defining the terms "collective security" and "cooperative security."[11] The purpose of collective security is a general one: it is an arrangement for deterring aggression through counter-threat and defeating aggression if it occurs. Cooperative security, on the other hand, is an arrangement for preventing such threats from arising, and for making preparations for them more difficult. Within this context cooperative security can integrate military and non-military components into a comprehensive security regime that can organize responses to possible sources of conflict. Clearly cooperative and collective security are mutually reinforcing. A fully developed cooperative security framework would include provisions for collective security as a residual guarantee to its members. The Conference on Security and Cooperation in Europe (CSCE) proclaimed the general principles of cooperation by its members in the Paris Charter, in November of 1990.

One can safely state that we should strive toward the emulation of the European CSCE model as our ultimate goal. Starting institution-building parallel with the on-going peace negotiation—as preparation for the stage when bilateral and multilateral agreements and treaties are signed—is of the utmost importance. For what will be the final nature of the Middle East peace process, and how we can establish, maintain, sustain and manage guarantees in the long-term needs to be discussed now. These essential requirements point to the importance of establishing a stable environment for the region through the creation of institutions and mechanisms for security and cooperation in the Middle East. That is, there is a need for some form of a Conference on Security and Cooperation in the Middle East (CSCME). One such institution could be a conflict prevention and crisis management center. The center could be a forum for political dialogue between states in the region; initiate studies of possible sources of conflict, thereby providing early warning; and facilitate the settlement of disputes in a peaceful manner.

In conclusion, arms control is only one dimension in the ultimate aim of establishing strategic stability and a "cooperative security" regime in the region. Other elements such as democratization, human rights, demography, economic, environmental and political cooperation play an equally important role. Multilateral institutions can reinforce a cooperative security arrangement.

NOTES

1. *SIPRI Yearbook on World Armaments and Disarmament, 1992* (Oxford: Oxford University Press, 1992), 320.

2. "Invitations to the Madrid Middle East Peace Conference," *U.S. Department of State Dispatch* 2:47.

3. "Organizational Meeting for Multilateral Negotiations on the M.E." *U.S. Department of State Dispatch* Vol. 3, Supplement 2 (February, 1992).

4. Secretary of State Baker, "Concluding Remarks at the Organizational Meeting for Multilateral Negotiations on the Middle East," op. cit., 28.

5. Alan Platt, "Introduction," in Alan Platt, ed., *Arms Control and Confidence Building in the Middle East* (Washington, DC: U.S. Institute of Peace Press, 1992), p. 3.

6. Sergey Koulik, "The 'Sinai Experience'" in Richard Kokoski and Sergey Koulik, eds., *Verification of Conventional Arms Control in Europe* (Boulder: Westview Press for SIPRI, 1990).

7. Richard Darilek and Geoffrey Kemp, "Prospects for Confidence and Security Building Measures in the Middle East," in Alan Platt, ed., *Arms Control and Confidence Building in the Middle East* (Washington, DC: U.S. Institute of Peace Press, 1992), pp. 9, 25.

8. Alan Crawford, "Verification of Disarmament or Limitations of Armaments: Instruments, Negotiations, Proposals," in Serge Sur,

ed., *The Armaments Lifecycle and Verification* (Geneva: UNIDIR, 1992).

   9. Ibid.

  10. Ibid.

  11. Ashton B. Carter, William J. Perry, and John D. Steinbruner, "A New Concept of Cooperative Security," *Brookings Occasional Paper* (Washington, DC: The Brookings Institution, 1992).

3   Arms Control and Confidence-Building in the Middle East: Policy Recommendations in Three Phases

Michael D. Intriligator

INTRODUCTION

The major global changes of recent years and, in particular, the advent of the Middle East Multilateral Talks have created unprecedented opportunities for arms control and confidence-building in the Middle East of a type and on a scale that would have been previously unimaginable. These new possibilities for arms control and confidence-building in the region can be realized through various initiatives, whether unilateral, bilateral, or multilateral. The purpose of this chapter is to explore these new possibilities via a phased agenda for arms control and confidence-building in the region. This new agenda represents a set of 22 substantive recommendations for the arms control and confidence-building component of the Multilateral Talks. It involves three incremental phases, starting with 12 initial actions, which are either unilateral or multilateral in nature; then three reciprocating actions, which are largely bilateral in nature; and finally seven major actions, which are largely multilateral in nature. The implementation of some or all these policy recommendations could significantly promote arms control and confidence-building in the region, leading to the possibility of a concept of regional security being achieved in the Middle East.

ARMS CONTROL AND CONFIDENCE-BUILDING

To start with definitions of terms, *arms control* will be taken here to mean military, security, and other initiatives, whether unilateral, bilateral, or multilateral, that reduce the chance of war or other military threats to regional security or that reduce the destruction caused by war or the costs of war. Arms control is not an end in itself but rather is a means to the end of regional security. Thus, the agenda for arms control must be driven by the perceived current threats to regional security rather than being fixed by history or traditional approaches to arms control. *Confidence-building* will be taken here to mean political, economic and other initiatives, again whether unilateral, bilateral, or multilateral, that can improve the relationships among nations in a region and thus create the conditions for peaceful development. Such measures must not undermine the security of the nations in the region, and they must be acceptable to all participating nations. Confidence-building provides the preconditions for arms control and various other types of cooperation, including military, security, political, economic, social, technical, and any other forms of cooperation among nations in the region.

Various types of arms control and confidence-building measures could be applied to the Middle East region. In general, they build on prior such initiatives in the region; in the East–West context; or in the post-Cold War world. They include initiatives that relate to weapons, delivery systems, communications, warning and surprise attack, accidental or inadvertent war, and arms shipments to the region. Some precedents for the region itself include the Tripartite Agreement, which, from 1950 until 1955, had successfully limited arms exports to the region; the 1978 Camp David agreement, which led to the 1979 Egypt–Israel peace treaty; and the stationing of observers in the Sinai to provide early warning and a political tripwire. Some precedents from the East–West context of the Cold War include the SALT and START negotiations and treaties on strategic arms reductions; the Conventional Forces in Europe (CFE) agreement on limiting conventional weapons in Europe; the Intermediate Nuclear Forces (INF) treaty eliminating an entire class of weapons; the Limited Test Ban treaty; the hot line; and the Stockholm agreement on the advance notification of military exercises. Some precedents from the post–Cold War world context include the North Atlantic Cooperation Council (NACC); the Chemical Weapons Agreement; and agreements pertaining to economic cooperation, including the establishment of various free trade areas. Thus, the negotiators at the Multilateral Talks could use the prior history of the region, the Cold War, and the post-Cold War world to help develop an agenda for arms control and confidence-building in the region. Such an agenda would build, in part, on earlier regional experience and the experience of other parts of the world, but it must be modified to take account of the present realities of the region and the current threats to regional security.

While some of the arms control and confidence-building experience from the East–West context might be applied, in suitably modified fashion, to the Middle East, it is also true that some of the experience in this region might conversely be applied to other regions. The end of the Cold War has made the world, (and in particular Eastern Europe and the former Soviet Union) more like the Middle East, with many actors, shifting alliances, historical antagonisms, disputes over territory, substantial minorities from one nation residing in another, wars, and occupied regions. Thus, the historical experience of the Middle East may be a window on possible future developments in (among other places) parts of the former Yugoslavia and parts of the former Soviet Union. Just as the breakup of the Ottoman Empire and the end of the British and French involvement led to conflict in the Middle East, so has the breakup of Yugoslavia and the Soviet Union led to conflict.

A NEW CONCEPT OF COMMON SECURITY FOR THE MIDDLE EAST REGION

Various policy initiatives could play an important role in establishing a new concept of security for the Middle East region. This new concept of security for the region would replace the current concepts of "national security" in the region. Newer types of weapons, along with the interdependence and integration that stem from developments in communications and transportation, have made it impossible to confine security to arbitrarily defined national frontiers. under current conditions, security is not an independent phenomenon but is rather inherently interdependent. Security must be defined from a broader perspective, and a useful perspective is that of the region rather than the nation. In particular, the concept of *regional* security should ideally replace the traditional concept of "national security." All parties in the region should take the position that security is gained not at the expense of another state in the region, as in a zero-sum game, but rather in conjunction with the security of these other related states, as a fundamentally positive-sum phenomenon. Security must be seen as a type of international public good, where more security for one nation does not diminish the security of other nations. In earlier periods, national security was frequently given as an example of a public good, a type of good for which one person's consumption of more national security does not diminish the level of national security for another person. Currently, however, this type of interpretation should be given not at the national level of individual people but rather at the international level of groups of nations in a region (or even at the global level) Thus, regional security is a type of international public good for which one nation's consumption of more security does not diminish the security of another nation.

Just as security must be looked at from a regional (rather than an individual and national) perspective, in terms of substance, the concept of security must extend well beyond its traditional military and political dimensions to include the interrelated military, political, economic, environmental, and other dimensions of security. Common regional security involves a complex web of interdependencies that require cooperation as the behavioral norm, with nations in the region cooperating in the interests of containing costly and dangerous regional arms races and resolving destructive regional conflicts. An important mechanism to achieve regional security is that of cooperation, where cooperation among the states of a region in relatively less controversial areas could be used as the basis for expanded cooperation in other areas, including arms control and security matters.

THE GRIT APPROACH

The question then arises as to how regional security in the Middle East region can be attained. One possible approach is initiating cooperation on smaller and less controversial areas and then building on them, as in the GRIT approach proposed in 1960 by the social psychologist Charles Osgood for improvements in East–West relations. GRIT, meaning "Graduated and Reciprocated Reductions in Tensions," involves initial steps that are reciprocated by larger steps, finally leading to major changes. It entails bargaining with an adversary without loss of advantage and without forgoing options before realizing a major agreement via small initiatives, which, if reciprocated, can lead to larger ones. In this instance, the initial steps, those of the first phase in arms control and confidence-building in the Middle East region, are unilateral or multilateral in nature but can cover a range of issue areas, involving diplomatic, political, military, economic, and other types of initiatives. The reciprocating responses, those of the second phase, are largely bilateral in nature and can also cover a wide range of issues. Finally, the major changes of the third phase are largely multilateral in nature and cover many areas of concern.

The rest of this chapter will focus on these three phases, each of which involves a specific set of substantive policy recommendations for arms control and confidence-building in the Middle East region. They involve various unilateral initiatives of or bilateral and multilateral agreements among the seven major actors represented in the negotiations: Israel, Egypt, the Palestinians, Jordan, Syria, the United States, and Russia. Other actors are omitted here, including Lebanon, Saudi Arabia, Iraq, and Iran, but they could also play a role in some of the initiatives or agreements proposed here. While the policy recommendations all involve some combinations of these actors, in many cases they require major new initiatives or departures by one of the actors and, in that sense, are largely unilateral in nature. In fact, unilateral initiatives could play a most important role in establishing the basis for later bilateral and multilateral initiatives. In that sense, they may be the most important measures for confidence-building in the region, providing the atmosphere for further steps of a bilateral or multilateral nature. The history of the region suggests the importance of such unilateral initiatives, particularly those that involve major discontinuities from the past. Examples include President Sadat's November 1977 visit to Jerusalem and President Carter's role in the 1978 Camp David agreement.

As suggested by the GRIT approach, the policy recommendations are organized into three phases: initial steps, which are relatively less controversial; followed by reciprocating steps; and ultimately leading to major policy initiatives. In general, the group of initial steps of Phase One provides the basis for a move to Phase Two, while the group of reciprocating steps of Phase Two provides the basis for a move to Phase Three, although some of the specific initiatives in any one phase could also be undertaken in earlier or later phases.

Phase One: Twelve Initial Steps for Arms Control and Confidence-Building

Some of the most important initiatives that could be taken for the purposes of arms control and confidence-building in the Middle East region, as already noted, are largely unilateral in nature, involving the initiative of one of the nations in the region or an influential nation outside the region. Some multilateral steps might also be undertaken initially as long as they are seen as being in the interest of all the parties. Twelve initial steps would constitute Phase One in the process of arms control and confidence-building for the region. Some or all of them could be taken by the major actors, either unconditionally or predicated on others taking comparable actions. Any group of them could provide a basis for moving to the next phase, although they are mutually reinforcing and interconnected rather than distinct, so the more of them that are taken the greater the likelihood of advancing to Phase Two. The twelve initial steps are:

POLICY RECOMMENDATION 1:

Israel should clarify its future role in the region, in particular, its relations with the Arab states and its current attitude toward the land-for-peace formula. (See the Postscript to this Chapter).

Israel is a pivotal actor in the region, so it is especially important that it clarify how it sees its role in the region. In particular, Israel should clarify what it would like to see as its future role with its neighbors and its current attitudes toward the land-for-peace approach used in the Camp David agreement and the possible relevance of this approach to both the occupied territories of the West Bank and Gaza and the Golan Heights.

Such a clarification could be done alone or jointly with comparable clarifications on the part of other actors in the region. In either case, this clarification could start a process of mutual understanding among all the actors in the region.

POLICY RECOMMENDATION 2:

Egypt should clarify its future role in the region, in particular, its relations with Israel and its role in the peace process.

Egypt is another pivotal actor in the region, so it is important that it clarify how it sees its future role in the region, including its future relations with Israel and its possible role in the peace process. It should clarify its view on the possible value of its existing peace treaty with Israel as a precedent for other nations of the region. Again, such a clarification could be done alone or jointly with comparable clarifications on the part of other actors in the region. As in the case of Israel, this clarification by Egypt could start a process of mutual understanding among all the actors in the region.

POLICY RECOMMENDATION 3:

Syria should clarify its future role in the region, in particular, its relations with Israel and its involvement in Lebanon.

Syria is yet another pivotal actor in the region, and the involvement of Syria in negotiations involving Israel is a most important development. To build on this foundation, it will be necessary for Syria to make clear how it conceives its possible future relations with Israel, in particular, the nature of the peace that it suggests might be possible if Israel were to return the Golan Heights under the formula it has proposed, namely "total peace for total return." It will also be necessary to clarify the relations between Syria and Lebanon and, in general, how it conceives of its future in the region, the nature of the peace that it envisages for the region, and the future relations among states of the region. Once again, such a clarification could be done alone or jointly with comparable clarifications on the part of other actors in the region, and, again, it could lead to mutual understanding and reciprocation.

POLICY RECOMMENDATION 4:

The Palestinians should clarify what they see as their future in the region, including their relations with Israel and the Arab states. (See the Postscript to this chapter.)

The issue of the Palestinians continues to be a major one which requires resolution. The Palestinians should clarify their position on what they envisage as their future in the region, including their future relations with Israel and the Arab states. Once again, such a clarification could be done alone or jointly with comparable clarifications on the part of other actors in the region, and it could lead to mutual understanding and reciprocation.

POLICY RECOMMENDATION 5:

Israel should make some initial steps in granting some measure of local autonomy in the West Bank and Gaza. (See the Postscript to this chapter.)

Some initial measures aimed at giving local autonomy in the West Bank and Gaza could be valuable as a signaling device to the Palestinians and to the Arab states that Israel is moving toward a resolution of the issue of the future of these occupied territories. It would be particularly effective if coupled with the Israeli clarification of its future role in the region, as in Policy Recommendation 1.

POLICY RECOMMENDATION 6:

The United States should play an activist and dynamic role in fostering confidence-building and arms control in the region.

The United States is the main foreign power affecting the region in the wake of the Cold War, the dissolution of the Soviet Union, and the Gulf War. It has good relations with both the

Arab states of the region and with Israel. Among other points of contact, Israel and Egypt are the two largest U.S. foreign aid recipients. The United States plays a major role as host and co-convener of the negotiations, but it must do more than act as a host or even a catalyst. It must take major initiatives in making proposals and work with all parties at the talks and outside the formal framework of negotiations to reach advances and agreements, including the adoption by the various parties in the region of the other Policy Recommendations of Phase One. A historical model and precedent for the activist role that could be assumed by the United States is that of President Carter in the 1978 Camp David agreement, where the United States showed dynamic leadership in helping the parties to the conflict reach a new agreement. The United States should also continue to work with Russia in continuing the formal framework of the negotiations.

POLICY RECOMMENDATION 7:

Israel should clarify its situation with regard to nuclear weapons and other weapons of mass destruction, including their means of delivery, and make precise the condition under which such weapons would be used.

The traditional Israeli approach is that of ambiguity or denial with regard to its having nuclear weapons, sometimes referred to as "covert" or "opaque" proliferation. Thus, its officials continually state that Israel "will not be the first to introduce nuclear weapons into the region." This approach can no longer be acceptable in view of the accumulated evidence of Israeli nuclear capabilities. South Africa has openly admitted that it had developed a small number of nuclear weapons and claims to have destroyed them. Israel should be similarly open about its capabilities, where such openness could itself be valuable as a contribution to greater transparency in the region. It should admit its nuclear capabilities and indicate the conditions under which such weapons would be used, presumably as weapons of last resort. It could also, in the process of admitting its capabilities, declare that it will be closing the Dimona facility, having sufficient fissile material for retaliatory weapons of last resort. As a first step, Israel could open the possibility of inspection of the Dimona facility, even without admitting having nuclear weapons, perhaps under the guise of seeking improvement in the area of nuclear safety. This could in itself be a valuable confidence-building measure, which could lead to arms control measures in the region. Israel might eventually see the value of limiting nuclear weapons in the region through adherence to the Nuclear Non-Proliferation Treaty (NPT) and the establishment of a Middle East nuclear weapons free zone if it perceives that Iran and Iraq could emerge as nuclear powers, opting for nuclear arms control as a way of curbing other potential nuclear powers in the region. until this happens, however, it is probably not realistic to consider the possibility of a nuclear weapons free zone in the Middle East.

POLICY RECOMMENDATION 8:

Egypt and Syria should each clarify their situation with regard to chemical weapons and other weapons of mass destruction, including their means of delivery, and make precise the condition under which such weapons would be used.

If Israel is open about its capabilities with regard to weapons of mass destruction, then so too should Egypt and Syria be open about their capabilities. If any of these three major actors admits its capabilities in this area, the others should follow. As in the case of Israel, such openness could itself be valuable as a contribution to greater transparency in the region. Traditionally the Arab states have declined to sign an agreement on chemical weapons because these are seen as weapons of last resort, playing a similar role in Arab states to the one nuclear weapons play in Israel. Changes in the Israeli position on nuclear weapons might lead to changes in the Arab position on chemical weapons. As to a possible chemical weapons free zone, just as it is probably not realistic to consider the possibility of a nuclear weapons free zone in the Middle East until Israel sees the value of limiting such weapons in the region, it is probably not realistic to consider the possibility of a chemical weapons free zone in the Middle East until Egypt and Syria see the value of limiting such weapons in the region.

POLICY RECOMMENDATION 9:

Egypt, Syria, Jordan, and Israel should reach agreements on advance notification of military exercises and on the concentration of military forces above certain agreed threshold levels, on the presence of observers at such exercises, on direct communications, on incidents at sea, and on advance notification of missile firing tests.

These agreements could defuse potentially explosive situations and avoid hair-trigger reactions and possible misperceptions. They could build on corresponding agreements reached in the East–West context, particularly the Stockholm agreement of the Conference on Security and Cooperation in Europe (CSCE) on advance notification of military exercises or concentrations of troops above threshold levels and the inclusion of observers in such exercises in Europe. Another precedent would be the hot line agreements on direct communications links between East and West. Third parties, including the United States and Russia, possibly with the participation of other nations and the United Nations, could help facilitate the provisions of these agreements, including the collection and dissemination of information on military movements and deployments, on incidents at sea, and on missile firing tests. Some of the technology that was used to install secure direct communications links between the United States and Russia could be used in the Middle East.

POLICY RECOMMENDATION 10:

Egypt, Syria, Jordan, and Israel should reach agreements on measures to reduce the risk of accidents involving weapons of mass destruction and conventional weapons.

These agreements could avoid the risk that accidents could lead to the outbreak of war in the region. As in the case of the previous policy recommendation, such agreements could build on corresponding agreements reached earlier, in this case by the United States and the Soviet Union. Of particular relevance are the 1971 Agreement on Measures to Reduce the Risk of Outbreak of Nuclear War and the 1973 Agreement on the Prevention of Nuclear War, calling for notification of any accidents involving such weapons that could lead to accidental or inadvertent war and urgent consultations in times of crisis to prevent unintended escalation. Conflict prevention centers could be established in all four capitals, possibly with third party observers or facilitators, for exchange of information, for notifications that would be required on agreements or confidence-building measures, and for control of escalation in case of a crisis.

POLICY RECOMMENDATION 11:

The United States and Russia, together with the other major arms-supplying nations of the united Kingdom, France, and China should set limits on arms transfers to the region.

After the Gulf War, in May 1991, President Bush proposed some limitations on arms transfers to the Middle East, but such limits were never established. Some limits are necessary for arms transfers to the region, building on the 1991 meetings in Paris and London and the 1992 meeting in Washington. The alternative would be a situation in which the Middle East becomes the major repository for weapons produced worldwide. A good starting point would be with the five largest arms exporters, who are also the five permanent members of the United Nations Security Council: the United States, Russia, the united Kingdom, France, and China. Any one nation would not have an incentive to control its arms trade, due to the activities of the other nations and to the profit, foreign exchange earnings, and employment-creation effects of arms exports. These major arms-exporting nations could, however, as a group, take the lead in setting limits on arms transfers to the region. An important precedent for limiting arms shipments to the Middle East region was the 1950 Tripartite Agreement, an agreement among the major arms suppliers of the region at the time (the United States, the united Kingdom, and France) which regulated the quantities and qualities of arms shipped to the region until the emergence of the Soviet Union as another major regional arms supplier (in its arms deal with Egypt in 1955). Some aspects of this agreement could be incorporated into a new "Quintipartite Agreement," involving the five current major arms suppliers to the region. In addition, it would be important to follow up an agreement among those five with subsequent agreements involving third-world arms suppliers, including Brazil, India, and Argentina. The United Nations Register of arms transfers would help in the implementation of setting limits on such transfers by providing an information base in this area. Advanced technologies for arms control developed in the East–West context could also be deployed in the region to determine the inflow of advanced weapons and the technologies to produce weapons of mass destruction. Agreements on limiting arms transfers should, of course, take into consideration the indigenous weapons production in the region and the effects of limits on transfers of such production on the security of the states affected.

POLICY RECOMMENDATION 12:

The United States and Russia, together with the other major nations supplying nuclear facilities and material, including the united Kingdom, France, China, Germany, and Italy should limit the transfer of materials to the Middle East that could lead to additional nuclear nations in the region, particularly Iraq and Iran. They should also take steps to limit the transfer to the region of materials that could be used in the manufacture of chemical weapons and other weapons of mass destruction and in the manufacture of missiles and other means of delivery of such weapons.

Additional nuclear weapons states in the Middle East would greatly complicate arms control initiatives and steps toward security in the region and could result in nuclear weapons being used in the region. Some of the nuclear capabilities of Iraq were destroyed by the 1981 Israeli raid on the Osirak reactor near Baghdad and again by the allied forces in the Gulf War, together with the activities of the United Nations following this war. Nevertheless, there remains the possibility of nuclear weapons in Iraq, if not now, then in the future. There also appears to be renewed interest in nuclear weapons in Iran, reestablishing the program that had been started under the Shah. The nations that export nuclear facilities should work to prevent the acquisition of nuclear weapons by both nations as such weapons would constitute a severe threat to security in the region, both in threatening each other and in threatening Israel and the Arab states. The nuclear supplier states should take unilateral initiatives to prevent the export of materials that could be used in a nuclear weapons program, and they should work in a multilateral way to tighten export controls through the Nuclear Suppliers Guidelines and the NPT, particularly to prevent further proliferation in the Middle East region. Similarly, these nations should take unilateral and multilateral initiatives to prevent the further proliferation of chemical weapons and missile capabilities in the region. The Australia Group could be involved in the regulation of the production and the stockpiles of chemical weapons in the region. Similarly, the Missile Technology Control Regime could assist in the regulation of the production of missiles and the transfer of missile technology in the region.

Phase Two: Three Reciprocating Steps for Arms Control and Confidence-Building

Some or all of these initial unilateral and multilateral steps should be followed by reciprocating steps that are largely bilateral, involving joint actions or agreements, explicit or implicit, among two of the nations in the region. Three such reciprocating steps constitute Phase Two in the process of arms control and confidence-building for the region. As in the case of Phase One, the adoption of a group of these steps would be interconnected and mutually reinforcing and would constitute a basis for the advance to Phase Three. The three reciprocating steps of Phase Two are:

POLICY RECOMMENDATION 13:

Egypt and Israel should determine a future for their bilateral relationships, including political, economic, and diplomatic cooperation that would be mutually beneficial.

The 1979 Egypt–Israel peace treaty is intact, but it has not created the possibilities for full cooperation between the two most important states in the region. Developing the relations between these two pivotal states, involving the most important bilateral relationship in the region, would be an important step toward regional security. It would be part of confidence-building, and it would indirectly support arms control for the region. The 1967 and 1973 "Hot Wars" between Egypt and Israel had been transformed into a "Cold War," while the peace treaty has further transformed the "Cold War" into a "Cold Peace." This current "Cold Peace" must be transformed into a "Warm Peace" through steps that would improve the bilateral relations between these nations. Cooperation between Egypt and Israel should extend over many areas of shared concern. Political cooperation should include more frequent meetings, particularly summit meetings of heads of government. Economic cooperation should include joint projects and relatively more open borders, allowing for movements of goods and services and also of labor and capital and other factors of production. Diplomatic cooperation should include shared initiatives for the region, particularly initiatives that could improve security for both, such as the prevention of terrorism. A historical model for the role of joint Egypt and Israel initiatives might be that of President Sadat's November 1977 visit to Jerusalem, where he was welcomed, thereby breaking an impasse through direct action.

POLICY RECOMMENDATION 14:

Israel and Jordan should determine a future for their bilateral relationships, including a peace treaty and political, economic, and diplomatic cooperation that would be mutually beneficial. (See the Postscript to this chapter.)

Jordan and Israel should work together to formulate and ratify a peace treaty, comparable to the Egypt–Israel peace treaty. Such a treaty would be a major step toward regional security. Jordan and Israel should also take other steps to improve their bilateral relations, including cooperation in political, economic, and diplomatic matters. These steps would, as in the case of comparable steps for Egypt and Israel, represent confidence-building and would indirectly support arms control for the region. Such cooperation could build on the model of improved Egyptian–Israeli cooperation.

POLICY RECOMMENDATION 15:

Israel and Syria should determine a future for their bilateral relationships, including a peace treaty and political, economic, and diplomatic cooperation that would be mutually beneficial. The return of the Golan Heights to Syria should be the basis of a peace treaty, as was the case of the return of the Sinai to Egypt, and some of the same mechanisms for security used in the Sinai should be used in the Golan Heights.

Just as Jordan and Israel should work together to formulate and ratify a peace treaty, comparable to the Egypt–Israel peace treaty, so, too, should Syria and Israel move toward taking this and other steps to improve their bilateral relations. Such cooperation, along with bilateral agreements between Israel and Egypt and between Israel and Jordan would provide a foundation for regional security. Steps to be taken in this area could build on the model of Egyptian–Israeli relations, in particular, on the precedent of the land-for-peace formula which was the basis of the Egypt–Israel peace treaty. A Syria–Israel peace treaty could follow from a return of the Golan Heights to Syria. Fortunately, in the case of the Golan Heights there is no dispute that this territory belongs to Syria, but the return of this strategically important region could create problems of security for Israel. Some of the mechanisms used in the case of the return of the Sinai to Egypt could well be used in the case of the return of the Golan Heights to Syria. These mechanisms used in the Sinai include manned and unmanned observation and detection posts; early warning stations in designated areas; ground, air, and naval patrols and on-site inspections; and other technical means to determine any potential violations of the border or demilitarized zone, with information on such potential violations transmitted to both sides. Another useful precedent is the experience of United Nations on-site challenge inspections of Israeli and Syrian forces in the Golan Heights since 1974. United Nations aerial photographic coverage of the Sinai, which had been extended indefinitely in 1975, should be expanded to cover the Golan Heights and other relevant borders of Israel. In addition, some of the technical means could utilize the high technology means for surveillance perfected by the United States or the Soviet Union during the Cold War, including satellite reconnaissance. A regional system of warning satellites providing information to all states in the region could significantly reduce the chance of surprise attack. Some of the newer ground-based technologies could be tested in the Sinai for possible use in the Golan Heights and possibly also in the West Bank and Gaza.

Phase Three: Seven Major Policy Initiatives for Arms Control and Confidence-Building

The major policy initiatives that could be taken for the purposes of arms control and confidence-building in the Middle East region would follow from these initial and reciprocating steps. They are largely multilateral in nature, involving joint actions or agreements among several of the nations in the region or nations playing a role in the region. As before, they are mutually reinforcing and interconnected, not distinct. Seven such major steps would constitute Phase Three in the process of arms control and confidence-building for the region. They represent the culmination of the steps taken in Phases One and Two, and some or all of them would be supportive of regional security for the Middle East. The seven concluding steps of Phase Two are:

POLICY RECOMMENDATION 16:

Egypt, Syria, Jordan and Israel should take joint initiatives for multilateral cooperation in a wide variety of areas, including economic activity, water resources, the environment, and the prevention of terrorism.

These initiatives could involve or lead to cooperation between Israel and its neighbors for mutual benefit in areas of common concern, including joint economic projects, the development of water resources, actions to preserve the environment, the treatment of refugees, and combined activities to prevent terrorism in the region. Such cooperation would reinforce other steps taken to ensure regional security. The funding for the joint projects, that would benefit all parties, could come, in part, from a fund for regional development administered by a regional development bank. A regional payments union would guarantee that net trade balances are paid in a convertible currency, thereby facilitating trade and investment in the region. Greater economic cooperation should be a step toward greater integration of the regional economies, which would be advantageous to all participating states of the region.

POLICY RECOMMENDATION 17:

Egypt, Syria, Jordan, Israel, and the Palestinians should make commitments to resolve their disputes via international arbitration or mediation.

International arbitration or mediation could play a valuable role in resolving disputes between and among the parties in the region. By providing an alternative to conflict or terrorism, peaceful dispute settlement would make a contribution to regional security. A precedent was the successful arbitration between Egypt and Israel over Tabra. Other disputes over territory or other matters could similarly be resolved through international arbitration or mediation.

POLICY RECOMMENDATION 18:

Israel, along with the Palestinians, Egypt, and Jordan should determine a future for the occupied territories of the West Bank and Gaza that is acceptable to both its own population, to the people of the territories and other Palestinians, and to the neighboring states in the region. (See the Postscript to this chapter.)

This determination of a future for the West Bank and Gaza is perhaps the most important initiative that Israel can take in confidence-building for the region and in establishing the conditions for arms control and regional security. The current conditions provide a favorable setting for such a step in view of the current sentiment in Israel moving in this direction, at least for Gaza if not for both the West Bank and Gaza, and the atmosphere created by the multilateral talks. The future of these territories would presumably involve a substantial element of autonomy and local control over most affairs and would not exclude the involvement of various Palestinian political groups, especially the PLO. It should not exclude the possibility of a state of Palestine, possibly in an economic union with Israel or Jordan or both. It should also allow for protection of certain Israeli settlements and for certain guarantees allowing for the defense of Israeli security. Clearly it will be a great challenge to find a solution acceptable to both Israelis and Palestinians, but such a solution is essential for further progress in all aspects of the negotiations. It should be facilitated by the bilateral discussions taking place between the Israelis and the Palestinians, but it is clearly up to the Israelis, as the occupying power of the territories, to determine their future. The current situation, which has existed since 1967, is not a viable one, and it has been a constant source of problems for all parties in the region.

POLICY RECOMMENDATION 19:

Israel and the Palestinians should build on the Israeli determination of a future for the West Bank and Gaza so as to strengthen their bilateral relationships. (See the Postscript to this chapter.)

Once the issue of the occupied territories is settled in a reasonable way, Israel and the Palestinians should work together to improve their bilateral relations in areas of common concern, including economic cooperation and cooperation in other areas. Cooperation between Israel and the Palestinians and their strengthened bilateral relationships would be a most important confidence-building measure for the region and would provide the basis for arms control and regional security.

POLICY RECOMMENDATION 20:

Egypt, Syria, Jordan, and Israel should reach agreements on open skies in the region, allowing overflights by nations of the region, other nations, or international bodies.

Allowing overflights in the region would make a major contribution to transparency, reduce the chance for surprise attack, and increase confidence. Some of the technical aspects of the agreement on open skies, as established in the 1992 Open Skies Treaty, could be employed in the Middle East region.

POLICY RECOMMENDATION 21:

Egypt, Syria, Jordan, and Israel should reach agreements and make commitments on reducing military spending, with the agreements monitored by international agencies. Resources freed through reduced military spending could be redirected to civilian use, with some part of the saving allocated to a fund for regional development.

These nations, particularly Syria, Jordan, and Israel, spend among the highest proportions of GDP on military expenditures worldwide. While each might be reluctant to cut military spending substantially, they might as a group reach an agreement to do so, particularly if there were independent monitoring of compliance with such an agreement, possibly coupled with security guarantees from outside parties. Reduced military spending would lower tensions in the region and reduce military capabilities, thus contributing to regional security. Labor, capital and other resources released from reduced military spending could be redirected to peaceful purposes, in particular, such resources could be used for building physical, human, and social overhead capital, including plant and equipment, facilities for education and health care, and communications and transportation systems. A fund for regional development should be established through each of the parties contributing some fraction of the amount saved on military expenditures, e.g., ten percent of the savings. This fund would finance joint projects to benefit all parties in the region, including economic and environmental projects. The United States could play an important role in taking the lead on creating a regional plan for the transfer of resources set free by reduced military spending to national and regional nonmilitary programs. A model for this U.S. role might be the Marshall Plan, under which the European countries receiving assistance were required to develop detailed plans on how they would make use of the resources provided under the plan. Given the substantial foreign assistance the United States provides to Israel and Egypt, it could, as it did in the case of the Marshall Plan, use its assistance as an incentive to encourage not only reduced military spending but also commitments to freer trade and economic cooperation in the region by conditioning further aid on such policies and the formulation of detailed plans for their implementation.

POLICY RECOMMENDATION 22:

The parties involved in the current negotiations, Egypt, Syria, Jordan, the Palestinians, Israel, the United States, and Russia, should develop a permanent regional organization for security and confidence-building. Such an organization might be patterned after the Conference on Security and Cooperation in Europe.

There should be a permanent organization created to ensure security and confidence-building in the region, thereby institutionalizing the other steps taken toward regional security. It would have a small Secretariat which would identify issues of concern and also opportunities for cooperation in various areas. There should be regular summit meetings of the parties at the heads of government level with ministerial level planning meetings to address these issues of concern and opportunities for cooperation.

CONCLUSION

These three phases of initiatives for arms control and confidence-building in the Middle East region, using the GRIT approach of graduated and reciprocated reductions in tensions could play an important role in achieving regional security. Clearly some of the 22 policy recommendations are more difficult than others, and some will take some time to be achieved, but they represent a possible agenda for new initiatives that could be taken, whether on a unilateral basis or on a bilateral or multilateral basis.

POSTSCRIPT

This chapter was completed in June 1993, prior to the Israel–PLO agreement of September 1993. That agreement might be interpreted, in terms of this chapter, as part of Phase One, the initial steps for arms control and confidence-building, in particular, as the fulfillment of Policy Recommendations 1 and 5 for Israel and Policy Recommendation 4 for the Palestinians and as a step toward the fulfillment of Policy Recommendations 18 and 19 for Israel and the Palestinians. Similarly, the Israel–Jordan agreement of October 1993 might be interpreted as a step toward the fulfillment of Policy Recommendation 14 for Israel and Jordan.

4   Arab–Israeli Arms Control and Confidence-Building Measures

Mark A. Heller

The purpose of this analysis is to examine the prospects for Arab–Israeli arms control and confidence-building measures (CBMs) in the context of the current peace negotiations and to venture some thoughts about measures that might be implemented in advance of peace agreements. Before proceeding, two important *caveats* should be stressed.

The first is that full-blown arms control agreements, meaning far-reaching constraints on the size and equipment of military forces, are highly unlikely in the best of circumstances, meaning a comprehensive peace settlement based on the resolution of the major outstanding political issues. Even then, the multiplicity of threats (some of them emanating from states not involved in the peace process), the ever-growing range of firepower, and the ambiguity of regional borders will make the search for such a regime exceedingly complicated, far more so than in the European context. Consequently, the focus here is on possible near-term measures involving Israel and its Arab neighbors (including those not participating in the multilateral talks). Such measures can comprise the basis for more ambitious security arrangements associated with possible peace treaties (particularly with reference to the military disposition of territories from which Israel might withdraw), but a full treatment of those issues is beyond the scope of this chapter. In short, we are primarily concerned here with CBMs rather than with structural arms control, and we view the purpose of such measures as twofold:

1. to reduce potentially dangerous military instabilities; and

2. to help produce a political environment more congenial to the search for peace agreements.

Second, we deal in this analysis largely with military CBMs, particularly with technical-military measures, i.e., with artificially contrived limitations on the deployment and training of military forces (sometimes referred to as operational arms control) and with political-military CBMs, i.e., declarations of intent concerning the planned use of forces and/or weapons. We do make limited reference to the rest of the universe of CBMs, which includes a variety of diplomatic, economic, cultural, and humanitarian initiatives implied in unilateral concessions and "goodwill" gestures, because such measures, by consciously encouraging the other side to accept a more benign view of one's own long-term intentions, also help to alter the psychological context of negotiations and conflict resolution. Indeed, some historical studies place conciliatory diplomacy at the very center of the confidence-building process.[1] However, the limitations of such measures should be acknowledged: while the perception of the adversary's ultimate intentions is a critical element of national security, measures that influence perceptions and affective views have no direct impact on the uses one may or may not make of military forces.[2]

THE NEED FOR CBMS

The immediate purpose of confidence-building measures is to alter the psychological framework of a relationship marked by deep mutual mistrust and suspicion of the other's elementary worldview. Psychological change is intended to promote two more concrete objectives: enhancing near-term security by reducing the danger that misperception and miscalculation may lead to uncontrolled escalation in situations of uncertainty or tension and creating a security environment than can facilitate conflict resolution, which is hampered by lack of confidence in the durability of any agreement that might be reached. In other words, CBMs aim to replace destabilizing expectations with stabilizing expectations.

To meet this aim, CBMs must address specific insecurities, at both the declaratory and the operational levels of military policy. The major insecurity in the Arab–Israeli arena is the spectre of a surprise attack, with the consequent incentive for each side to attack first itself. Confidence-building can reduce this incentive if it is operationalized to mean *both* enhanced trust in the other side's intentions (reassurance) *and* sustained faith in one's own capacity to cope with the consequences of trust which may turn out to have been misplaced (deterrence).

MECHANISMS FOR BUILDING CONFIDENCE

Effective change in expectations will best proceed from a change in declaratory posture regarding *intentions*. Explicit renunciation of the first use of force is clearly a vital foundation for the process of confidence-building. In and of itself, a declaration of this sort cannot truly assuage fears, because the very existence of a conflictual relationship causes even the most solemn declarations to be at least partially discounted. Nevertheless, the building of mutual confidence in intentions will be very difficult without a declared commitment to pursue a settlement of conflicts through peaceful means, abjuring both the *use* and the *threat* of force.

Beyond that, confidence-building means intensifying trust in the sincerity and credibility of this commitment while retaining self-confidence in the ability to deal with defection. Declaratory posture, if sustained and reiterated over time, can certainly contribute to that process. In the Arab–Israeli case, for example, Jordan has so consistently declared its commitment to a peaceful settlement of the conflict that Israelis have come to take Jordan's pacific long-term intentions almost for granted, so much so that when Jordanian statements or actions, such as hostile propaganda, border incidents, and even participation in Arab war coalitions, appeared at variance with that commitment, Israelis were quick to look for mitigating circumstances to explain Jordan's "reluctant" or "involuntary" belligerency. This stance can be—and is—ascribed to the peculiar character and vulnerabilities of the regime, and there is concern in Israel (akin to apprehensions about future political developments in Egypt) that Jordan's posture *vis-à-vis* Israel might be repudiated by a radical successor regime claiming to represent the country's "authentic" personality. Nevertheless, these concerns do not negate the basic point that perceptions of the adversary's intentions, even in a continuing state of war, can be influenced significantly by declaratory posture and other CBMs such as direct communications, especially if these measures are seen to conform with the declarer's vital interests.

At the same time, even the most reassuring statements of intentions need to be reinforced by conscious, voluntary measures to constrain *capabilities* in the military sphere, because only concrete actions of the sort that effectively reduce attack options enhance both types of confidence:

1. trust that the adversary intends to do (or not to do) what he says he intends to do (or not to do)—in this case, not to attack; and,

2. belief in the ability to deal with the consequences of failure to conform with declared intentions, normally by ensuring preservation of the means at least to frustrate if not punish any attempted attack.

Jordanian capabilities before 1967 were in any event bounded by the country's limited population and resources. Nevertheless, Jordan buttressed its general posture of non-belligerency by eschewing operational coordination with other Arab countries and refraining from stationing armored forces in the West Bank until shortly before the Six-Day War, and Israel was able to monitor Jordanian behavior and detect any deviation from that policy early enough to take countermeasures. In short, constraints on capabilities, defined as "prohibitions on military activities that are significant, easier to define, and relatively easy to verify,"[3] reduce the fear of surprise attack because they reduce the possibility of surprise attack; explicit measures to limit attack options provide a material test by which to evaluate the sincerity of reassuring declarations of non-aggressive intent.

There are, of course, many kinds of CBMs that can convey the earnestness of one's intention to comply with declared intentions. The most obvious is to provide hostages to good behavior. Long before the term CBM was coined, rulers sent relatives or other high-ranking personages to reside in the court of potential adversaries; the expectation was that these emissaries would be killed if their master violated an undertaking to refrain from aggressive action. It was this logic that led Israel to attach such importance to the reopening of the Suez Canal and the reconstruction of Canal-side cities by Egypt after 1973; this is also why Israel views with such apprehension Syria's refusal to repopulate Kuneitra after its restoration to Syrian control in 1974, notwithstanding the fact that the cease-fire itself has been scrupulously respected.

However, most discussions of CBMs, especially those inspired by the Helsinki/Stockholm model in Europe, now focus on measures specifically related to the equipment, organization and preparation of armed forces. Since we have assumed that significant changes in the material attributes of armed forces will have to await peace agreements, our immediate concern is with what might be termed the operating systems and software of military forces: doctrine, procedures, intelligence/operational security, deployment, training, and planning. In operational arms control, these elements are purposely fashioned to discourage worst-case assumptions by providing testable assurances of non-aggressive intent. The purpose is to reduce ambiguity or broaden the margin of tolerable ambiguity by consciously enhancing the adversary's early warning and increasing the time available for him to prepare, thereby minimizing the prospect that an attack could succeed. Since both sides know that the other is better able to deal with an attack, either through defense or retaliation, the measures in question presumably build the confidence of both sides that a surprise attack will not occur.

This objective is pursued in a variety of ways.[4] One assumption driving the case for confidence-building through operational arms control is that while camouflage, deception, and artifice are good for war-fighting, they are bad for war-preventing (provided, of course, that what is revealed cannot be exploited by the other side to increase his own offensive capabilities). Many of the practical proposals put forward in this realm therefore relate to *transparency*, i.e., enhancing each side's knowledge of what the other is doing or planning to do by disclosing that which military forces traditionally try to conceal. Thus, CBMs call for such things as publication of data concerning orders-of-battle and procurement programs and prior notification of the time, scale, nature and location of planned troop exercises and weapons tests. Of course, voluntary release of information cannot eliminate suspicions of deception, and transparency also means facilitating the adversary's ability, independently or through credible third-parties, to verify the accuracy and comprehensiveness of information through electronic and physical observation and on-site inspection. Antecedent or associated measures, such as military-to-military contacts, direct communications networks and joint work in crisis control centers, can also contribute to reassurance through *socialization*, presumably because the de-demonization of the adversary helps to diminish insecurities stemming from worst-case assumptions. Third, reassurance can be given through adoption of certain *rules or norms* concerning the non-threatening nature of normal military activities, such as limits on the size of military maneuvers or their proximity to borders and on the trajectories of aircraft training missions and missile tests.[5] In addition, warning time can be increased by *physical separation* of opposing forces, frequently buttressed by the presence of international "peacekeeping" forces. Indeed, in the record of CBMs in the Middle East, buffers and demilitarized or limited-forces zones are by far the most prominent element. Finally, political-military leadership may announce adoption of reassuring changes in *military doctrine*, although any actual reconfiguration of forces to conform with doctrinal changes will have to await decisions about structural arms control.[6]

ARAB–ISRAELI EXPERIENCE WITH MILITARY CBMS

Many of these measures were adopted at one time or another in the Israeli–Arab relationship; physical separation measures have been particularly prominent. For example, acceptance of the cease-fire agreements of 1949 involved the establishment of U.N. Truce Supervision Organizations, Mixed Armistice Commissions and several demilitarized zones and pockets of "no-man's land," and the cease-fire in 1956 was followed by the creation of a United Nations peacekeeping force—UNEF I—in Sinai. Short-term stabilization considerations also came into play in the 1974 Egyptian–Israeli and Syrian–Israeli disengagement-of-forces agreements and in the creation of a

UNIFIL-patrolled zone in southern Lebanon following the Israeli incursion (the "Litani Operation") in 1978.[7] However, the limited degree of cooperation that emerged has had a decidedly mixed record in terms of advancing the ostensible objectives of CBMs. Demilitarization of the Sinai and the presence of UNEF after 1956 did not prevent the outbreak of the Six-Day War in 1967; UNIFIL did not prevent an Israel–PLO mini-war of attrition in the summer of 1981 and an Israeli invasion of Lebanon the following year; and the informal Syrian–Israeli "red-line" agreements limiting the geographical scope and character of Syrian military involvement in Lebanon (following Syrian intervention in the Lebanese civil war forestalled neither a crisis over Syrian missile deployments in 1981 nor large-scale Syrian–Israel combat a year later.[8] Indeed, such measures sometimes produced a psychological environment even less conducive to the resolution of the conflict. Thus, if confidence-building measures are defined by the objectives they promote rather than by their technical specifications, there may be grounds for questioning whether the measures constituting the Arab–Israeli experience really qualify as CBMs at all.

It might be postulated that the shortcomings of these CBMs stem from their mechanical insufficiencies, i.e., that they have been too few and too modest. However, that explanation begs the prior question of why more numerous and ambitious measures were not undertaken. The answer to that question would seem to lie in the origin and context of decisions taken— particularly the close connection with active fighting that had taken or seemed on the verge of taking a highly undesirable turn for the Arabs. Most of the CBMs recalled in the Arab–Israeli experience were actually a function of very short-term calculations. Arabs accepted them (or simply did not object to their implementation by third parties) as the price to be paid in order to stop the fighting and maintained them for prudential reasons (i.e., only as long as they were effectively deterred from defecting, rather than as part of a conscious effort to reassure

Israel about non-belligerent intentions over the long term); Israel accepted CBMs as partial compensation from third parties for its agreement to stop fighting and/or withdraw, but in the face of essentially unchanged threat perceptions, it continued to rely for its security on military deterrence, which inevitably implied a element of threat to the Arabs. Consequently, the basic structure of the relationship remained unchanged and the limited CBMs that were instituted could hardly promote the larger purposes that CBMs ostensibly serve.

The major exception to the pattern described above was the second Egyptian–Israeli Disengagement Agreement of 1975. Sinai II was qualitatively different from other CBMs in several ways. until the breakthrough Israeli–Palestinian and Israeli–Jordanian agreements of September 1993, it was the only Arab–Israeli agreement not fashioned simultaneously with or directly after the termination of active fighting for the limited purpose of stabilizing a military front; instead, it was formally linked to the negotiation of a final peace agreement. Moreover, it explicitly referred to the future intentions of the parties concerning the use of military force by incorporating a clear renunciation of the threat of use of force in the pursuit of a political settlement. In this sense, Sinai II was not just a military CBM but a political-military CBM, and its significance lay not so much in the operational constraints on offensive options, especially surprise attack capabilities (though these were far from inconsequential) but rather in the authoritative disavowals of intention to use force, which the operational constraints reinforced. Sinai II did not incorporate renunciations of further Egyptian claims against Israel, but it did codify an Egyptian undertaking not to pursue those claims by military means. The centrality of these commitments to pursue a peaceful resolution of the conflict and "not to resort to the threat or use of force or of military blockade" is underscored by the fact that they are contained in the first two articles of the Agreement.[9]

Of course, the undertaking itself could not produce total Israeli confidence that the commitment would be honored. However, the declaratory dimension was an important condition of the ambitious military stabilization measures associated with the Agreement, which included extensive limited armament and buffer zones and a major American role in the verification provisions. Moreover, the package incorporated additional political CBMs, such as an Egyptian agreement to passage of "nonmilitary cargoes" for Israel through the Suez Canal, a partial easing of the secondary boycott, and a moderation of anti-Israel propaganda, thereby improving the psychological environment for conflict resolution. In short, the significance of Sinai II was that it was an explicit mutual security pledge, grounded in recognition that "armed conflict was no longer an effective means of achieving political and strategic objectives."[10] This kind of cooperation/reassurance in security matters still fell far short of convergence on political and strategic objectives, but it provided the psychological foundation for movement toward conflict resolution which was beyond the reach of the modest, incremental military CBMs adopted until then.

SUGGESTIONS FOR FUTURE CBMS

Sinai II is a powerful precedent in two respects: it suggests the importance of measures divorced from arrangements to terminate active fighting, and it demonstrates the impact of declaratory measures. Indeed, it might be argued that the prospects for significant Arab–Israeli progress on other fronts depends on the extent to which the Egyptian–Israeli pattern, *mutatis mutandis*, can be replicated.

The Syrian case is particularly critical, since Syria is the strongest Arab force confronting Israel and the Syrian–Israeli military relationship, though not necessarily the most volatile, would produce the most destructive consequences if a clash did occur. By the same token, the political consequences of diplomatic progress facilitated by CBMs are also likely to be most far-reaching. For a truly significant political-military CBM to be possible, Syria must explicitly endorse the conclusion reached by Egypt: that the military option is not viable over the near or long term. Syrian willingness to renounce the threat and use of force probably depends, to some extent, on the belief that reassurance, military stabilization, and an embryonic posture of security cooperation will not be interpreted by Israel as strategic surrender, i.e., that these measures will not have the effect of guaranteeing perpetuation of the territorial status quo. Even more important, however, will be Syria's conviction that the current stalemate is undesirable and that there is no reasonable prospect of changing it by other means.

It is not yet clear that Syria has reached this point, since the evidence that can be adduced is ambiguous. On the one hand, the Syrian government has entered into direct peace negotiations with Israel and, in contrast to previous practices, has tentatively begun to prepare opinion for the possibility of peace in ways that have been noticed by the Israeli analytical and policymaking communities, if not yet by the general public. From these actions, it is possible to infer that Asad has concluded that international developments such as the collapse of the Soviet Union and the Gulf War have rendered a military option nonviable and that the need for a "peace dividend" has grown more urgent. On the other hand, Syria continues to host the most radical factions of the PLO, to tolerate if not encourage the activities of Hezbollah in Lebanon, to maintain close ties to Iran, and to pursue a major buildup of military forces; these actions can be explained by Syria's traditional determination to maintain options as long as possible (especially, as in the case of Iran, when there are few more attractive alternatives) and to maximize Syrian influence over other Arab actors, especially in Lebanon. But they may also reflect a calculation that the current standoff is neither intolerably painful nor unacceptably dangerous as well as a lingering belief that the desire to avert war will determine Israeli policy with respect to the Golan Heights.

Even without a Sinai II-type commitment, Syria could undertake a variety of CBMs in order to reduce the ambiguity surrounding its policy. Indeed, a modest Syrian–Israeli military CBM regime already exists, and this may provide the basis from which to proceed to more ambitious and politically potent measures.

In the area of *transparency and predictability*, for example, it could agree to establish a routinized direct military-to-military communications channel, for which there is a historical precedent in the form of the Mixed Armistice Commission.[11] The ability to exchange unmediated, real-time information might help forestall the emergence of crises from unanticipated directions. Second, the risk that unanticipated problems might arise could be reduced by elaborating a set of *rules and norms* or "agreed procedures" with respect to the behavior of military forces. Again, political obstacles might be surmounted by relying on existing precedents, in this case, the Israeli–Syrian "red-line" agreements. These understandings could provide the basis for a commitment by the two parties not to use Lebanese territory for military attacks against the territory of the other.

Beyond Lebanon, one idea which suggests itself for early consideration because it is relatively uncontroversial is an understanding about the behavior of naval forces patterned on the US–Soviet "incidents at sea" agreement. Indeed, it would be useful to discuss the overall issue of dangerous military activities, perhaps in a working paper of the bilateral negotiations. In this forum, for example, the parties might undertake some explicit agreements with respect to the trajectories for missile tests and aircraft training missions. Third, the parties could experiment with inspection and verification procedures by agreeing to send and accept national representatives to the U.N. force (UNDOF) monitoring the disengagement and limitation of forces agreement on both sides of the lines on the Golan Heights. (By the same token, Israel and Lebanon could agree to attach joint observer teams to the UNIFIL force operating in southern Lebanon.) Based on the principle of gradualism, such measures could provide the basis for more formalized confidence-building procedures (such as prior notification of military exercises) and institutions (such as a permanent conflict prevention/crisis management center) at a later stage.

Such measures would have only a limited impact on the stability of a robust cease-fire regime that has already passed several severe tests and would directly address only the issue of the *unintended* use of force. Nevertheless, they would also constitute a political signal and thus contribute, if only indirectly, to the reduction of insecurities concerning the *intended* use of force that pose the most serious obstacle to a political settlement. For CBMs to have a greater impact on these types of insecurities, they will have to incorporate a weightier political component. One example of political-military CBMs of this sort could be a publicized agreement on the use of military and paramilitary forces for non-military missions, e.g., cooperation in search-and-rescue or anti-smuggling operations. Such a measure would have virtually no impact on military capabilities *per se*; its significance lies precisely in its non-military character, i.e., as a concrete if modest manifestation of Syria's agreement to include Israel in the rubric of what Mikhail Gorbachev, in his elaboration of Soviet new political thinking, called "universal human concerns."

The same calculus indicates the potential contribution of direct communication with the adversary's population (even for avowedly propagandistic purposes), even though this sort of CBM has even less of a military component in it. Syria's boycott of Israel has historically been so absolute that Syrian governments have not even bothered to try misleading or demoralizing, much less reassuring Israeli public opinion. Like other measures potentially available, a Syrian effort to address directly the Israeli public, perhaps through the medium of an interview with Asad by an Israeli journalist invited to Damascus for that purpose, would not constrain Syrian military options, but it would have a perceptible impact on Israeli confidence, if only because of its very novelty. This sort of initiative might be more feasible precisely because it would be less far reaching (though, for that reason, less potent) than the blanket Egyptian commitment to abstain from the first use of force undertaken by Sadat in 1975.

CBMs appear to be governed by an inverse (and perverse) relation between urgency and feasibility: the more they are needed, the less they are possible. If this is so, it should be easier to implement more far-reaching measures in other sectors, where Israeli–Arab military relations are less dangerous, where arms control and CBMs has been explicitly endorsed (at least in principle) through participation in the multilateral negotiations, and where—at least insofar as Egypt and Israel are concerned—a formal state of peace already obtains. Indeed, the Egyptian–Israeli case offers some particularly promising possibilities because there is an existing CBM regime which does not need to overcome political obstacles associated with problems of recognition and legitimacy. It should not be difficult to publicize the workings of the security arrangements annexed to the Egyptian–Israeli Peace Treaty, including the routinized liaison between Egyptian and Israeli forces, and to intensify or initiate other forms of military-to-military contacts, such as reciprocal visits to military academies, training exercises, etc. Such measures could reinforce public confidence in both countries and also provide a kind of field test for consideration by others.

In addition, the Egyptian–Israeli dyad could serve as a basis upon which CBMs involving Israel and Jordan, Saudi Arabia, and perhaps Yemen could be developed. The most appropriate mechanism might be a regional arrangement—a Red Sea Crisis Management Center, perhaps based somewhere in the Sinai— which could provide a forum for direct communications to clarify questionable activities by naval and air forces in the area and to coordinate search-and-rescue operations involving civilians and military personnel.

Finally, while the structure of the multilateral negotiations does not lend itself to operational agreements, it is well suited to the exploration of conceptual issues and the elaboration of broad guidelines. In this context, the multilateral forum might usefully establish a working group to discuss, define and specify "Dangerous Military Activities." The objective of this working group would be to identify confidence-building constraints on the scope or character of routine activities by land, sea and air forces and to suggest mechanisms for dealing with accidents or unexplained actions which might cause misunderstanding, retaliation or escalation. Examples of possible subjects include the accidental or unauthorized entry of armed forces of one party into the territory of another, collisions or near-misses between naval vessels or aircraft of the parties involved, and interference with military communications or early-warning systems. Although a "dangerous military activities" working group might start out as an "academic exercise," its conclusions and recommendations could quickly be adapted and implemented, when political conditions permit, in a variety of bilateral or sub-regional settings.

NOTES

1. See, for example, Kevin N. Lewis and Mark A. Lorell, "Confidence-Building Measures and Crisis Resolution: Historical Perspectives," *ORBIS*, 28:2 (Summer, 1984), 281–306.

2. Hence, non-military CBMs on their own neither enhance nor diminish confidence in the likelihood of an attack by the adversary. Perhaps the most dramatic non-military CBM in the Arab–Israeli context was the visit to Israel by Egyptian President Sadat in November 1977. But at least one high-level Israeli official—the IDF Chief of Staff—insisted that the impending visit was actually a trick

aimed at lulling Israel into a false sense of confidence and urged a higher state of military alert. Anwar el-Sadat, *In Search of Identity* (New York: Harper & Row, 1978), p. 309.

3. Richard E. Darilek and Geoffrey Kemp, "Prospects for Confidence-and Security-Building Measures in the Middle East," in Alan Platt, ed., *Arms Control and Confidence Building in the Middle East* (Washington, DC: United States Institute of Peace, 1992), p. 23.

4. The variety of possible measures is described in greater detail by Thomas Hirschfeld, "Mutual Security Short of Arms Control," and Yair Evron, "Confidence Building in the Middle East," in Dore Gold, ed., *Arms Control in the Middle East*, JCSS Study No. 15 (Tel Aviv: Jaffee Center for Strategic Studies, 1990).

5. For some suggested missile-related CBMs, see Mark A. Heller, "Coping with Missile Proliferation in the Middle East," *ORBIS*, 35:1 (Winter, 1991), 26–28.

6. For a detailed discussion of the Soviet doctrine of "non-offensive" or "defensive defense," see Stephen M. Meyer, "The Sources and Prospects of Gorbachev's New Political Thinking," *International Security*, 13:2 (Fall, 1988), 124–63.

7. Many of these measures are reviewed in Indar Jit Rikhye, "The Future of Peacekeeping," in Gabriel Ben-Dor and David B. Dewitt, eds., *Conflict Management in the Middle East* (Lexington, MA: Lexington Books, 1987), pp. 261–68.

8. The first of these understandings, worked out with U.S. mediation, established a southern limit to Syrian operations. In 1978, a second "red line" was tacitly drawn around the Christian stronghold in Mt. Lebanon and east Beirut. Syria was also expected to refrain from using air power or deploying air defense missiles in Lebanon. However, an incident in 1981 was interpreted by Israel as a violation of the "air power" rule and Israeli reaction led to a crisis in the summer of 1981 which was temporarily defused but ultimately resulted, at least in the view of some analysts, in the Israeli invasion in 1982. On the "red line" agreements, see, Zvi Lanir, *Israel's Involvement in Lebanon: A Precedent for an "Open Game" with Syria?*, CSS Paper No. 10 (Tel Aviv: Center for Strategic Studies,

April, 1981), 9–10. For more on Syrian–Israeli relations with respect to Lebanon, see Itamar Rabinovich, "Controlled Conflict in the Middle East: The Syrian–Israeli Rivalry in Lebanon," in Ben-Dor and Dewitt, eds., *Conflict Management in the Middle East*, pp. 97–111.

9. *The Quest for Peace: Principal United States Public Statements and Related Documents on the Arab–Israeli Peace Process 1967–1983* (U.S. Department of State, 1984), p. 62.

10. Brian S. Mandell, "Anatomy of a Confidence-Building Regime: Egyptian-Israeli Security Cooperation," *International Journal*, 45:2 (Spring, 1990), 203.

11. Arye Shalev, *Shituf Pe'ulah B'Tzel Imut* [Cooperation under the Shadow of Conflict] (Tel Aviv: Ma'arachot, 1989).

5   Innovative Proposals for Arms Control in the Middle East

Ahmed Fakhr

INTRODUCTION

Arms control, in its wider sense, is becoming more and more important in the Middle East since the Madrid Peace conference of October, 1991, as it has a direct impact on any and all peace steps in the bilateral negotiations between Syria, Jordan, Lebanon, the Palestinians, and Israel. Successes and progress in arms control negotiations, especially in the multilateral track, will help shape the acceptability of security measures needed to achieve bilateral peace. Indeed, the multilateral negotiations, which aim at reshaping post-peace regional security dynamics, have already made a great impact on all of the negotiation baskets—economic cooperation, water, environmental problems, and the refugee dilemma. All five multilateral baskets are mutually interrelated, as all have an impact on future security and stability in the region. Of course, security depends greatly on arms control.

Notwithstanding the increasing importance and attention paid to arms control, this chapter will not repeat the many sound proposals suggested in the many serious studies conducted by prestigious experts and scholars for research institutions and think tanks. Here, rather, we will try to dream, to innovate instead of imitate, and to explore and open vistas for new ideas and proposals.

THE GOALS OF ARMS CONTROL IN THE MIDDLE EAST

Discussion and negotiations on arms control in the Middle East do not occur in a vacuum. Rather, there is extensive previous experience to draw on, both European (especially American–Soviet) and Middle Eastern. Since the 1950s, the United States, the Soviet Union, and others have pursued a wide range of arms control measures aimed at reducing the risk of war while simultaneously preserving and promoting their respective national security. It is widely recognized that these two goals have often come into conflict and that usually the latter dominates. Indeed, many specialists seek to draw on the superpowers' experience for lessons—of both successes to be emulated and failures to avoid—that can be applied to the Middle East. I would like to suggest that such attempts, while useful, have significant limitations.

unlike the superpowers' experience, which focused on reducing the risks of war, the Middle East arms control process begun at Madrid aims at helping to make and ensure a lasting, comprehensive, and just peace. It should be noted that the American–Soviet experience showed that in an atmosphere of mutual suspicion and hostility, the process of negotiating a reduction in war was often the only area in which the two superpowers had been able to work together productively. We cannot say that this is the climate in the Middle East. Our recent history of wars and the accumulation of suspicion leads at least some of us to feel that improving the regional political environment is a prerequisite for successful and productive regional arms control measures.

Finally, the experience of more than four decades of conflict, instability, and wars has led the regional states to focus on procuring military equipment, thereby opening the door to a regional arms race—and all the dangers of instability that implies. Arms control is something new to the hearts and minds of people in the Middle East. Because of the relative novelty of arms control, it is very important to make sure that we are all speaking the same language, especially because there is confusion about the distinctions between arms control, arms limitations, arms reductions, arms embargoes, and disarmament. For the Arabs, arms control means the promotion of regional national security. Arms control ideally means promoting the national security of *all* regional parties, without discrimination, by limiting or reducing the threat posed by adversaries or neighboring countries and helping to ensure peace. That is, arms control is not a substitute for military preparedness but a supplement aimed at ensuring security and legitimate defense at lower and less dangerous levels. That is why arms control is a tool, a means serving regional goals.

Given the complexity of regional security in the Middle East, the goals of arms control must be ambitious. Among the major goals are:

- military stability;

- military transparency and predictability;

- crisis stability;

- prevention of proliferation;

- a reduction in the consequences of war if one occurs;

- a reduction in the cost of defense;

- and an improvement in political relations.

In terms of regional *military stability*, Egypt has focused on two major issues. The first is the introduction to the region of destabilizing weapons—weapons that can cause a decisive military outcome can lead to fundamental changes in the political and military environment. That nuclear weapons can cause such a fundamental change was recognized soon after the bombing of Hiroshima and Nagasaki in 1945. Because of their destructiveness, nuclear weapons are highly destabilizing. The second issue is the introduction into the region of weapons that provide specialized capabilities that enhance the ability of one country to create a dramatic change in the balance of military power. For example, providing Israel with a technological edge in order to ensure that the military balance is guaranteed to be in its favor is destabilizing as long as the military balance is defined as the comparable combat power of two parties or coalitions.

The importance of increasing *transparency* is based on the realization that an inability to detect the military capabilities of other states often leads military leaders to make "worst-case analyses" that create additional pressures for arms buildups—not arms control. The best solution for increasing regional *predictability* is for all parties to adopt the concept of transparency so that other regional parties will be aware of the respective national objectives, interests, and strategies. The lessons of recent experience with Iran and Iraq underline the importance of transparency. The Middle East is characterized by deliberate nuclear ambiguity, chemical ambiguity, and ambiguity about delivery systems and indigenous research and development as well as domestic military production. Israel, Iran, and Iraq are special cases here.

The importance of *crisis stability* is based on the recognition that achieving peace will not mean that all countries of the region will have the same national objectives, interests, and policies. The potential for differences and contradictions leading to problems and disputes will always remain. While we may hope that through peaceful agreements and adequate arms control measures and political dialogues we will be able to prevent problems from escalating into crises and military conflicts, in the meantime we should be very careful to prevent accidental war—or war by mistake. This could mean that the armed forces that are going to accept the elimination of destabilizing mass destruction weapons and unneeded provocative offensive equipment will have to be provided with special military capabilities to continuously monitor and appraise the regional situation in order to avoid crises, as well as military equipment to make the initial crisis assessment and notify the concerned regional parties to prevent a crisis. Among the possible tools to achieve this goal are hot lines and operational agreed upon restraints.

The fourth major goal of arms control is the *prevention of the proliferation* of nuclear weapons and associated delivery systems. Currently Israel's strategy is one of nuclear ambiguity. While this could barely be accepted when there were reports that Israel possessed eight to ten nuclear warheads (presumably as weapons of last resort should its existence be threatened), such a presumption *cannot* be accepted when there are now reports that Israel has 200–300 nuclear warheads. Militarily speaking, one needs 10–12 nuclear warheads to cripple an Arab country during a war. There are 22 Arab countries; 300 Israeli warheads are far more than is needed! The Middle East cannot accept Israeli nuclear monopoly. The disintegration of the former Soviet Union and Eastern Europe opened the door for Middle Eastern countries to seek to obtain nuclear warheads, delivery systems, raw material, scientists, nuclear research laboratories, and other forms of assistance. Addressing the goal of non-proliferation of nuclear capabilities should be a goal for all states in the Middle East, but it is also a global responsibility. The same holds for other weapons of mass destruction.

Reducing the cost of security and defense is a major and noble objective, especially as the Middle East has suffered from a long arms race and has paid an enormous price for the disastrous consequence of continuous conflict and war. The priority of the Middle Eastern states should today be economic, social, and peaceful technological development in order to join the advanced world and compensate for the suffering of the peoples of the region.

But there are two dilemmas in achieving the goal of reducing the costs of security and defense. First, while ultimately it is possible to reduce the financial burden of providing national security by limiting military spending and the unneeded destabilizing quality and quantity of weapons and forces, in practical terms arms control agreements did not save either the United States or Soviet Union significant sums of money *until* there were significant improvements in their political relationship leading to a drastic change in their mutual threat perception. Second, the Gulf War demonstrated a new era of ultra-effective conventional weapons, whetting the appetite of regional states to procure them, and suppliers to sell them.

The last, but certainly not least, goal of arms control is the *improvement of political relations.* While the relationship between arms control negotiations and political relations is complex and often unclear, in general progress in arms control efforts signals relative improvement in political relations. This is a lesson I have drawn from the multilateral talks between Arabs and Israelis. To be sure, the meetings in the multilateral working group on arms control have proven more important politically than in terms of actual results, which we are waiting to achieve. But one important function of the discussions has been to establish arms control as a central focus of the Arab–Israeli dialogue.

THE NEW ENVIRONMENT

The pursuit of these ambitious goals takes place in an environment that has undergone radical changes over the past few years, and it is an environment that continues to change. Indeed, it is the recognition that these goals are important that has led to efforts to ensure that the changes that occur are beneficial and stabilizing, not detrimental and destabilizing. In order to facilitate these efforts, we will discuss practical steps or measures that can help in achieving most or all of the goals previously identified. But first let us examine the changing environment.

In the Old World Order there were special rules that were tacitly known to parties involved in the Arab–Israeli conflict, which existed under the umbrella of the two superpowers. While the Soviet Union supported the major Arab confrontation states, since 1967 the declared and implemented American military relation with Israel was, and is, to guarantee its qualitative edge over the Arabs. This support was and is (albeit bitterly) accepted by the Arabs and was justified as it was undertaken in the context of the East–West conflict.

In the New World Order the situation has changed. The East–West conflict no longer exists in the wake of the collapse of the Soviet Union. So what was justified yesterday is no longer justified today. The United States should understand that not only is there a new international order but also a new Middle Eastern order. This order needs to be based on a new balance of interests, a new balance of power—without one party having military superiority or a qualitative edge. The United States should take the role of balancer in order to help any future steps in regional arms control.

While it is worthwhile for regional states to learn about arms control from external parties, drawing on their experiences, in exploring new and innovative steps the focus should be on the regional experience. In part this is because the environments are so different, in part because the old international environment—from which these lessons are drawn—no longer exists. In the Middle East there have been highly successful experiences in arms control measures, including the Israeli–Syrian disengagement agreement of April, 1974 as well as the consecutive Egyptian–Israeli agreements: the March, 1974 disengagement agreement, followed by the 1975 interim agreement, and finally the peace treaty of 1979. These precedents should provide suitable lessons.

One important step is to avoid double standards. We need to see the United States dealing with all Middle Eastern parties on an almost equal basis when it comes to the issues of arms control, human rights, internal legitimacy, and the condemnation of military aggression. It should no longer be the case that a regional party can say: "If we do not have the U.S. administration, we have the Senate; if we do not have the Senate, we have the House; if we do not have the House, we have our lobby or pressure groups." In foreign policy, and especially in terms of arms control and regional security arrangements, it is necessary to deal with a state, with the United States as a whole, not with parts of the United States contradicting other parts. This is the starting point of double standards!

SPECIFIC STEPS AND MEASURES

For a long time now the world has been trying to convince Israel to end its nuclear ambiguity and make an announcement about the nuclear weapons it owns. One cannot go on with the arms control process when one does not know what is to be negotiated or controlled. Rather than suggest that Israel declare what it does have, we here suggest that Israel declare what it *does not have*. For example, Israel could declare that it does not have nuclear mines, and this could help in accelerating an agreement on the withdrawal from the Golan Heights. Or Israel could declare that it does not have naval nuclear mines, thereby encouraging the parties to adhere to an agreement regarding incidents at sea. Or that it does not possess or will not use nuclear artillery, giving more credibility to prior notification of force movements. The more military stability, military predictability, and military transparency created in the region, the sooner some of the most important objectives of Middle East regional arms control can be achieved.

In order to improve regional political relations and increase stability and other important goals of arms control, it is essential that an annual "white paper" be published and distributed. Such a defense "white paper" could be unilateral, bilateral, or regional. It would include statements on and information about national and military objectives, interests, policies, and strategies, and defense expenditures. Such a "white paper" could be a new method of dealing with regional threat assessment; success in this kind of transparency would help in reducing the costs and consequences of wars.

Because official arms control negotiations sometimes face a deadlock and the intervals between official rounds are often long, informal and unofficial consulting groups from the various parties involved can be very helpful. Such meetings can help to overcome misunderstandings, generate new ideas, and ensure a continuing dialogue in between official rounds.

There are a number of other steps that can be taken in the arms control process. The development of a Middle Eastern Missile Technology Control Regime can help prevent proliferation. A regional computer database with information on defense industries military holdings, stockpiles, and new defense projects and research and development could increase transparency. Transparency and familiarity with the approaches of the various parties could also be increased by establishing a regional institute for security and defense cooperation and by publishing a regional defense journal to which all military personnel in the area could contribute. Holding unilateral and multilateral regional arms exhibitions open to all who wish to attend could serve the same goal, as could establishing regional environmental testing centers and regional control labs, facilitating regional mutual maintenance training, and creating defense–industrial participation and cooperation.

Any arms control agreement should be verified. The United States and the former Soviet Union used to depend on their highly advanced and sophisticated national technical means (NTM) of surveillance for verification. The establishment of a regional verification agency, using or hiring surplus American or Soviet NTMs should be an up-to-date method for verifying all regional arms control agreements. Such verification is crucial to ensure that all parties abide by the agreements—or are aware of any violation.

Finally, much work needs to be done on developing an international and regional plan for the conversion of the indigenous defense industry that is not needed for legitimate defense purposes into civilian economic production. Such conversion should be part of any plans for development assistance to the region, including any regional "Marshall Plan."

CONCLUSION

In this chapter we have explored ideas which would underpin long-term, specific arms control initiatives in the Middle East. To ensure practical implementation any innovative proposals for arms control in the Middle East should depend on some major elements, including:

- the belief of all parties concerned that all are working not to prepare for a coming war but to make peace possible;

- the understanding that success in arms control necessitates drastic changes in the existing regional political environment, and vice versa;

- the paradox that in spite of the impossibility of isolating politics from security, in arms control people in uniform should be more innovative and move as quickly as—even ahead of—the politicians.

Such a starting point will generate proposals which can lead to a lasting, comprehensive, and just peace.

Factors Affecting Arms Control and Regional Security

6 An Arms Control Regime for an Arab–Israeli Settlement

M. Zuhair Diab

INTRODUCTION

Given the long duration of the Arab–Israeli conflict and mutual fears, a security regime comprising an arms control regime should be created to facilitate and strengthen a settlement. For such a regime to function properly two basic elements are required: a territorial settlement and general deterrence. In order to assure the stability of deterrence and thereby underpin the settlement, an arms control regime is essential.

The bilateral and multilateral negotiations between Israel and the Arabs started after President George Bush's peace initiative of 6 March, 1991, and his proposal for arms control in the region on May 29.[1] The existence of two sets of negotiations and, specifically, their division into bilateral political and multilateral functional domains reflect the assumption that weapons and arms races are symptoms of conflicts and not their cause. Yet the multilateral talks on arms control are based on the assumption that certain weapons systems could be destabilizing.

Arms races may reinforce mutual threat perceptions among adversaries and may lead to preventive war.

The recognition that weapons and technological developments can destabilize an already precarious political–military situation led in the 1960s to the novel concept of arms control. Advocates of arms control recognized that while conflicts may persist among nations, a variety of policy measures can be adopted to reduce tension and curb arms races, thereby maintaining stability.[2] Indeed, arms control was a principal part of the policy of conflict management between the Western and Eastern Blocs until the demise of the Cold War and is still being pursued to control nuclear proliferation. It achieved relative success in reducing tension and reaching several agreements on capping the arms race and methods of crisis management.

Can such an approach, developed mainly in the bilateral relationship between the superpowers, be successfully applied in the context of the Arab–Israeli conflict? If so, how should it be implemented, taking into account the different conditions of the two strategic environments?

THE BASIC REQUIREMENTS

It should be emphasized at the outset that the parties to the Arab–Israeli conflict are still grappling with two major problems that deeply affect their relations: First, there is Arab dissatisfaction with the status quo of continued Israeli occupation of territories taken in the 1967 War and a zone in southern Lebanon since 1978; second, an acute security dilemma renders the security of one side to be the cause of another's insecurity. The combination of these two factors distinguishes the European environment from the Arab–Israeli one. A prescribed Arab–Israeli arms control regime or more limited arms control measures, aiming mainly to ameliorate the security dilemma, will have to go in tandem with serious efforts to settle the thorny territorial issues, the basis of Arab dissatisfaction.

A key concept in arms control is deterrence, especially nuclear deterrence. It is argued that by maintaining a certain posture of military force, a defender can prevent or dissuade a challenger from resorting to certain actions by influencing the latter's calculus of cost and benefit.[3] The validity of this assumption has been challenged on several grounds, particularly its basis in rationality. It has been demonstrated that deterrence could not only be challenged because of opportunity but also because of the pressure of political needs, regardless of the military balance. The criticism becomes stronger when conventional deterrence is the only one available.[4]

However, since the proposed comprehensive security regime for the Middle East rests on combining the strategies of general reassurance—which aims at minimizing the likelihood of antagonists resorting to threat or use of force through the establishment of security regimes, restraints and norms of behavior, and Graduated and Reciprocated Reduction in Tension (GRIT)—and deterrence, the shortcomings of a pure policy of deterrence are considerably remedied.[5] For an arms control regime in the Arab–Israeli conflict to have a realistic chance of success, there are several guiding principles that must be adhered to:

- Mutual general deterrence is a useful point of reference.

- The national security requirements of all members have to be met.

- Security has to be based on equality, not on superiority of one side at the expense of another.

- Military balances have to take account of the different mix of forces and the technological gap.

- Any cuts of restraints in the possession of certain types of weapons systems must be based on reciprocity, although this does not bar asymmetry and trade-offs.

- Time and gradualism are essential factors in introducing measures owing to deep-seated mutual suspicions.

- A comprehensive regime will be established when a comprehensive political settlement is in place.

- An effective verification system has to be installed to police and enforce the regime.

With these guidelines, it becomes fruitful to examine the major issues involved, as well as their relative importance and priority in order to recommend appropriate policy measures. While considerable attention has been given to how confidence- and security-building measures (CSBMs) may gradually contribute to decreasing threat perceptions and mutual suspicions (and under the right circumstances can be useful in complementing arms control measures), it must be stressed that the application of any measures—including CSBMs, arms control, or both—should be synchronized with progress in the political/bilateral negotiations and the implementation of steps agreed to in order to reach a final settlement.[6]

MEMBERSHIP

The membership of the proposed security regime, whether limited or comprehensive, will comprise Israel, Egypt, Syria, Lebanon, Jordan and a future Palestinian state, federated or confederated with Jordan. It has been limited in this way to avoid endless arguments over the geographical dimension of all possible threats. It is recognized that Israel could face a single or a combined threat from any of the Arab members or from outside the geographical confines of the regime. In order to consolidate the regime and address the Israeli concern about threats outside the regime, the Arab members will have to renounce any alliances directed against Israel once it has fully complied with the agreed political settlement. The same will apply to Israel. However, this condition should not restrict the freedom of any member to act outside the designated area of the regime. The Arab members, therefore, would be free to fulfill their obligations under the Arab League Charter of 1945 and the Treaty of Joint Defense of 1950 unless Israel is a victim of an unjustified attack by an Arab party.

CONFIDENCE- AND SECURITY-BUILDING MEASURES (CSBMS):

During the Cold War, CSBMs were proposed as measures to reduce tension, avert unwanted war through miscalculation, and prepare the ground for arms control agreements, especially on the conventional level. The central idea was to create confidence and clarify intentions among the adversaries in the West and East. The European model of these measures was mainly shaped in the Helsinki and Stockholm Agreements in 1975 and 1986 respectively.[7]

It has been suggested that this model could be transplanted partially or totally in the Arab–Israeli conflict even before a political settlement is initiated.[8] Such proposals overlook serious differences between the two environments regarding the nature of conflict and the status of the adversaries.[9] By the time CSBMs were introduced in Europe, the two blocs in the Cold War became more or less satisfied with the status quo. The main concern was to avoid inadvertent war because of misunderstanding, accidents, and miscalculation, particularly during times of heightened tension in a crisis. The need for such measures became more urgent with the introduction of technologically advanced weapons systems. This concern with crisis stability combined with a permissive political climate in

Europe facilitated the degree of openness and transparency required by CSBMs.

As such conditions do not at present prevail in the Arab–Israeli conflict, it is very difficult to contemplate introducing wide-ranging CSBMs. Israel has not yet accepted the basic Arab demand of full withdrawal from the territories occupied in 1967. Accepting any CSBMs would place the Arab governments in an awkward position *vis-à-vis* their peoples, especially with the continuation of violence against the Palestinians. Moreover, the Arab side regards confidence-building as a part of its negotiating power. Militarily at a disadvantage and having lost the backing of the Soviet Union, the Arab side has been left only with the power of denial. Denying any form of cooperation with Israel, until it agrees to the Arab demands, is the optimal strategy available to the Arabs.

In a political climate which also does not see any substantial progress in the negotiations, CSBMs, which are basically a kind of legitimate spying, would end up heightening mutual suspicions instead of infusing confidence. In the Arab–Israeli environment, the introduction of CSBMs, without agreement at least on the outline of a political settlement, could be counter-productive.

To break out from this vicious circle, it might be very helpful if Israel made a commitment to eventual and full withdrawal, and, simultaneously, the Arab parties, especially Syria, committed themselves to enter into peaceful relations with Israel once a settlement is implemented. These acts are essential to establishing reassurance between the parties so that CSBMs could be introduced gradually to develop mutual trust and verify each others' peaceful intentions. The adoption of the various measures should be tuned to the needs of each front as the withdrawal agreements are being carried out. The main emphasis should be on measures that prevent surprise attack since preemption has gained a premium in the Arab–Israeli context. The CSBMs would be also useful in defusing border incidents, since dissatisfied political groups, on both sides, are likely to try to undermine the settlement. Such measures, if adopted, would form a limited security regime on their own, in case arms control proper proves difficult to realize in the short term.

There is extensive experience with CSBMs in the Arab–Israel conflict, including demilitarized and restricted deployment zones.[10] The United Nations also has a long experience in the region.[11] While important practical lessons can be learned from this experience, what is suggested here is a more comprehensive regime meant to buttress an enduring peace settlement, and not merely an armistice among belligerents, as was the case previously. The following list could be proposed:

- A summit by all the signatories to the peace treaties may create confidence and signify an effort to put aside the past.

- Israeli withdrawal can be phased over a period extending from one to five years, depending on the front in question. Such periods can allow the testing of intentions and the efficiency of the security measures.

- Satisfactory demilitarized and restricted deployment zones can be delineated to avoid frictions and act as a buffer against a surprise attack.

- The final peace agreements can be guaranteed by the U.N. Security Council, putting that body in charge of supervising their implementation and policing them.

- Joint political and military committees under U.N. chairmanship can be formed to supervise implementation of and deal with any breaches of the agreements.

- Joint military patrols can be formed to monitor compliance.

- Early-warning posts can be stationed on both sides of border, with mixed crews headed by a U.N. officer.

- U.N. disengagement forces can be deployed in the demilitarized zones with authority to prevent border incursions by paramilitary groups.

- A crisis management center can be set up in Jerusalem headed by a senior U.N. diplomat and helped by senior diplomats and military officers from the parties. The head of the center will also have direct contact with the foreign ministers of the parties.[12]

- Following the implementation of agreements, it is possible to connect the offices of head of states or governments with hot-lines.

- All members can accept satellite and aerial reconnaissance, whether by national means or by the permanent members of the U.N. Security Council.

- Advanced notice of military maneuvers exceeding divisional strength, or 12,000 soldiers, must be given within an agreed time to the respective joint committee.

- No party will permit the stationing of foreign troops without the prior approval of the U.N. Security Council.

- Each party has the right to request an on-site inspection in the demilitarized and restricted zones with the presence of a U.N. officer and without prior notice.

- Any movement of military forces that exceeds divisional strength, or 12,000 soldiers, for internal security purposes, or if requested by another party as assistance, must be reported to the respective joint committees and to the crisis management center within a reasonable time.

Not included in the proposed measures is the attendance by observers from the other parties of military maneuvers or conducting maneuvers jointly. Such a step requires a higher stage of military cooperation and even the final resolution of the conflict, and this stage may even obviate the need for security measures on the ground. One has to bear in mind that the Arab–Israeli conflict is not only among states but also between societies charged with all their national ethos. It will take a lot of effort and a considerable length of time to eradicate the antagonism and injuries inflicted by both sides upon each other. Still, small but steady first steps have better prospects of producing results than attempting to leap-frog realities.

CONVENTIONAL MILITARY BALANCE

Whereas CSBMs could be readily adopted given the appropriate political conditions, the questions of force structures, size, some types of weapons systems and doctrine could prove more problematic. The European experience in this area is not very encouraging, as no substantive agreement was achieved until the late 1980's, after the Soviet Union had started to disengage itself from Eastern Europe.[13]

Two fundamental problems hamper achieving easy and quick agreements on these issues. The first problem stems largely from the difficulty of reaching consensus on the definition of national security requirements. States and their leaders have widely divergent views on how to determine present and future potential threats. Moreover, it is natural for the government of the day not to commit future governments to obligations concerning the security of the nation that may prove fatal. Then, too, estimating the quantity and quality of military forces required to efficiently protect the national interests of every state and meet any contingency is not a simple and straightforward matter. Subjective bias and the intangibles of military capabilities impede fixing an objective yardstick on military postures. In addition to these complications, states have a tendency to seek to maintain an edge of military superiority against their present and potential opponents in order to be on the safe side—thereby creating a security dilemma.

Regarding the Arab–Israeli conventional military balances, these problems are compounded by the different levels of socio-economic development within Israeli and Arab societies. Israel is part of the technologically advanced Western world, while Arab societies, with some variations, are still struggling with the basic problems of economic and political development.

Israel, owing partly to the historical trauma of the Holocaust and partly to the deep feeling of distrust, has adopted a maximal security concept that couples territory with its ultimate security. Notwithstanding the acceptance of Israel's reality and legitimacy generally by the Arabs, or at least the Arabs directly involved in the conflict, Israel has not entirely divested its security from the territorial dimension. The point to be stressed is that both sides consider territory to be a security asset. While Israel is concerned about possible Syrian threats from the Golan or Lebanon, so, too, is Syria concerned by the fact that Israeli troops in the Golan are but 40 kilometers from the defense perimeter of Damascus and Israel could outflank Syrian defense in Lebanon. To these concerns must be added questions of historical rights and legitimacy. Consequently, a redefinition of Israel's basic security concept, decoupling it from the occupied territories, would be a breakthrough helping to overcome a major obstacle in achieving a minimum consensus on the national security requirements of all parties.

Size of Forces and Their Structures

If for Israel the main threat comes from a single or combined Arab attack, the problem for the Arab states is more complicated for two reasons: First, the Arab parties to the conflict are also involved in the inter-Arab strategic environment containing disputes that occasionally escalate to armed hostilities, as the experience of Iraq's invasion of Kuwait in 1990 demonstrated. Second, Arab armies have a prominent role in upholding the regimes in power. They serve as the ultimate means of violence that maintain internal stability. This is mainly because of the lack of strong political institutions that furnish legitimacy for the government of the day. In addition, the armed forces in Arab developing societies provide a sizable sector for employment. Hence, it is not unnatural for the Arab side, particularly Syria and Egypt, to resist major cuts in the size of their forces.

Clearly, this is not an argument to allo ● the Arab parties a free hand to build huge military machines if peace materializes. A reasonable ratio could be worked out which permits the members of the regional arms control regime to make sure that the size of their armed forces is predictable over time and under scrutiny. This ratio must take into consideration several crucial factors such as the external and internal security needs of each member, the process of modernization, the population pools, and the proportion between standing and reserve units. On this last point, it is futile to demand that the Arabs emulate Israel's reserve system, essentially because of the technological gap. On the whole, Israel has a tendency to exaggerate Arab military capabilities by quoting sheer numbers and stressing the high percentage of standing units.[14] This argument is not based on a sound analysis of the combat effectiveness and performance of Arab armies in the battlefield.[15] Thus, it is feasible to agree to certain flexible ceilings, reviewed periodically in light of political and technological developments.

As for force structures, particularly the distribution and mix among the various services, again it should not be made an obstacle to the development of an arms control regime since Arab armies have different doctrines, and they are far from mastering modern military technology. They have no alternative for the foreseeable future but to rely on their ground forces as their mainstay of defense in case deterrence fails. The essential rule for the regional arms control regime is to emphasize flexibility and openness to verify intentions, which are more important than capabilities in the context of an arms control regime in which the members are bound together in contractual peace.

The Arms Race and Advanced Weapons Systems

It is established as a generalization that arms races by themselves are not a direct cause of war.[16] However, in combination with other variables, in a conflictual situation arms races may facilitate the decision to go to war. The cardinal factor is, more often than not, political grievances. It is customary to point out that if two sides are in an adversarial relationship, and one side perceives that its opponent has accumulated enough armaments to tip the balance of power, the first side may resort to preventive war. The case of the 1956 War launched by Israel, joined subsequently by Britain and France, against Egypt is usually cited.[17] But even in that case there were factors in addition to the Czech arms deal with Egypt that created the conditions for war, including the closure of the Gulf of Aqaba, Egypt's encouragement to Palestinian infiltrators, and the nationalization of the Suez Canal. A state may also go to war if its opponent achieves a technological breakthrough that could empower it to inflict a strategic defeat. Nuclear weapons aside, it is very doubtful whether the parties in the Arab–Israeli conflict have the capability to reach this stage. Moreover, preventive war as a doctrine is no longer accepted internationally.

Nonetheless, since the objective is to stabilize the military environment and because the arms race constitutes a contributing factor to instability, it should be capped between the members of the regime. But such restrictions have to be within the criteria affecting force size and structure and should not affect the acquisition of advanced weaponry. In the last thirty years weapons and their systems have advanced beyond expectations.

Every system has been countered with another one that neutralizes its impact. Accuracy and firepower have been set as the guiding objectives behind research and development projects, bearing in mind the cost–effectiveness ratio. Any attempt to put the clock back is doomed to failure; to deny certain countries the state of the art in weapons technology is discriminatory and will not have a chance of success.

Expert opinions have been divided on whether advanced weaponry helps the defense or offense.[18] The experience from recent wars, especially in the Middle East, provides mixed answers. In the October War of 1973, precision-guided munitions (PGM) helped the Egyptians and Syrians to blunt the fist of Israeli armor in the initial stages while air-defense systems confused the superior Israeli air force until American electronic counter-measures (ECM) were supplied to Israel.[19] In the Lebanon War of 1982, the Israeli air force again demonstrated its superiority in suppressing the Syrian air-defense means and controlled the air.[20] However, this encounter should not be generalized, partly because the Syrian political leadership miscalculated Israeli intentions and did not take timely measures to strengthen Syrian positions[21] and partly because Israel only engaged air-defense points and not the integrated air-defense system inside Syria. The Gulf War against Iraq in 1991 clearly illustrated that technologically advanced weaponry can significantly help to shorten war and reduce civilian casualties. Yet after further investigations, conclusions are usually tempered about the rate of success achieved by these weapons and conventional wisdom prevails—namely, that tanks, airplanes and guns are still the mainstays in affecting a decision in the battlefield.[22]

But it should not be denied that the sophistication of and improvements in target acquisition techniques, artillery range and firepower, command, control, communications and real-time intelligence (C^3I), precision-guided munitions (PGMs), and electronic counter-measures (ECMs) have considerably enhanced the efficacy of conventional weapons. The question of whether they bolster deterrence and defense more than offense, or the other way round, is really dependent on other variables in a conflict. The basic variables are the intentions of the adversaries, their military doctrines, and whether both sides possess these weapons and in what quality and quantity.

Therefore, although the parties to the regional arms control regime are not supposed to resort to force in their relations, they should not be asked to forswear modernizing their weapons systems in order to defend themselves if the regime breaks down. Such modernization, particularly when the political problems are solved, will increase self-confidence and reduce the fear of a crippling surprise attack or loss of control in a crisis, which may motivate preemption. It should be noted also that arms control does not necessarily imply reducing every category of weapons systems. Some may have to be increased and modernized as the defensive needs of the state in question require. Jordan and Lebanon, for example, need to greatly improve their air defenses and the mobility of their ground forces. Syria still requires the replacement of at least half of its obsolete air force and tanks. Egypt has not yet completed the modernization of all its outdated major Soviet weapons systems.

This process of modernization and augmenting the defenses of all members of the regime ought not to frighten Israel if it is interested in a stable military environment. The acquisition of advanced weaponry must be dealt with in a contextual framework so as to create sufficiency in defensive postures. The insistence on maintaining a qualitative edge for Israel is not a recipe for stability for two reasons: First, it will fuel the arms race by encouraging the Arab side to seek quantity in order to make up for a high degree of qualitative disadvantage and, second, increasing the vulnerabilities of the Arab parties is not a recommended measure of arms control but rather a prescription for another war.

Military Doctrines

An area of arms control causing much controversy is whether military doctrines play a part in destabilizing deterrence. The difficulty occurs when a state claims to be on the defensive strategically but adopts an offensive doctrine tactically. Because of geography, structure of forces, or manpower, such a state maintains that it cannot afford to allow its opponent the advantage of a first strike; hence, the former has no choice but to regard preemption as a basic tenet of its doctrine.[23] The paradox is that every nation pretends to be defending its security when it is really defending an advantageous status quo, regardless of whether it is at the expense of another nation's security.

To put the matter in perspective, one has to look first at the political issue at stake; once it is settled the question of doctrine comes second. Sources of doctrine vary among states depending on a host of factors that form their overall strategic concept: historical, cultural, geographical, manpower, and economic resources are important in influencing doctrine. However, when a state stresses preventive war or preemption as a constant security policy under any circumstance, then it is undoubtedly displaying aggressive intentions. Clearly, such a policy does not help stabilize the military environment or strengthen deterrence as it generates suspicions of every military move or arms acquisition.[24] On the other hand, it would be unreasonable to demand from every state a unified military doctrine without taking into account its circumstances and the threats it might face. Hence, this issue should not be given priority in the envisaged regime between Israel and its Arab adversaries. The members ought to be encouraged to emphasize defensive doctrines, especially when CSBMs are in place to assist in averting an unwanted war through accidents or miscalculations and to give a timely warning of a surprise attack.[25]

Nuclear, Chemical and Biological Weapons

It has become customary to call nuclear, chemical, and biological weapons "weapons of mass destruction," adding to them medium- and long-range missiles.[26] The criteria set for such a classification apparently relate to their scope of destruction and the moral abhorrence they invoke whenever they are cited as threats or actually used. The first three categories have become the subject of international regimes.

The Treaty on the Non-Proliferation of Nuclear Weapons of 1968 (NPT) is based on a discriminatory principle between the original members of the nuclear club, the five great powers which have openly declared themselves as nuclear powers while other states have been asked to forfeit such possession. A few near-nuclear states, among them Israel, have so far refused to join it. The Arab states, on the other hand, seeing themselves in a technologically disadvantageous position, have all adhered to it, although Iraq tried unsuccessfully to develop a military nuclear program.

The central theme in the Israeli argument to keep its nuclear option open is that it needs a weapon of last resort since it is outnumbered by its enemies and that international guarantees are not reliable. However, Israeli leaders have always insisted that Israel will not be the first to introduce nuclear weapons in the Middle East, even though recent unconfirmed reports have indicated that it has manufactured a substantial arsenal.[27] The impact of Israel's nuclear program on the course of the conflict is open to debate. While it has been argued that nuclear weapons can convince the Arabs that Israel is indestructible, the 1967 War was more than instrumental in driving home this message. A presumed nuclear capability has failed to compel the Arabs to accept Israeli conditions for a settlement over the occupied territories. Moreover, it did not deter Egypt and Syria from launching the limited-liability war of 1973. Whatever the merits of the argument either way, it is very difficult to contemplate

Israel easily giving up the option it perceives as a reliable insurance policy.

The debate has acquired a new twist as the Chemical Weapons Convention (CWC) was opened for signature in 1993. Egypt, Syria, Jordan, and Lebanon have abstained from joining unless Israel becomes a member of the NPT and opens its nuclear facilities to international inspection by the IAEA, though Israel has signed the CWC.[28] The problem has become more complicated since Israel has extended the geographical scope of nuclear threats to include Iran and Pakistan, in addition to any Arab state such as Algeria, Libya, or Iraq before the Gulf War. The problem of nuclear proliferation in the Middle East has evolved into a circular one as each state shifts the responsibility upon the shoulders of another. Iran denies that it is developing a military nuclear option but points out that Pakistan and Israel have done so. Pakistan, in turn, accuses India of starting the nuclear arms race in the subcontinent. Kazakhstan now drags its feet on handing over to Russia nuclear arsenals left on its soil after the disintegration of the Soviet Union. All indications point to the conclusion that nuclear weapons or capabilities in the Middle East are going to stay with us for the foreseeable future. Consequently, the concept of a nuclear-weapon-free zone in the Middle East is simply out of date,[29] as nuclear proliferation should be treated on a global level.

President Bush's initiative contains some preliminary measures to curtail nuclear proliferation through banning the production of military fissionable nuclear materials and subjecting nuclear facilities to IAEA's inspection. While such proposals and others are worth consideration, it is very doubtful whether any could be implemented without a change in the political climate in the region. Although the picture is rather pessimistic as far as reaching a quick agreement on nuclear nonproliferation in the context of the Arab–Israeli conflict, there is no immediate danger of a nuclear conflagration. However, if Israel wants to retain its nuclear option, then it must accept the fact that Egypt and Syria do not intend to bargain away their possession of chemical weapons, whatever their military utility. The main inhibition on Israel's either using its nuclear capability or threatening to use it as a form of blackmail remains international constraints and the dangerous unforeseen consequences.

As for the Convention on Banning Biological Weapons of 1972, the Arab states have joined it, realizing the minimal military advantages of biological weapons in deterrence; Israel has not yet joined the Convention. This Convention, unlike the NPT and CWC, does not provide for an inspection system, which may keep adversaries uncertain about compliance.[30] In the end, it is the moral repugnance of these weapons that restrains states from threatening their use or actually using them. Still, if nations are cornered in militarily desperate situations, moral inhibitions may give way to employing any means to protect their survival.

In summary, progress in settling the Arab–Israeli conflict and proceeding with certain arms control measures should not be made dependent on achieving agreements on the above three types of weapons. This is because of the complicated nature of their control and the wider political and military issues they raise. Moreover, they are basically weapons for deterrence rather than for battlefield use. The use of chemical weapons in the war between Iran and Iraq is simply irrelevant to the Arab–Israeli context because of the threat of retaliation and the deep involvement of Western powers, particularly the U.S., in the conflict.

The territorial question is more pressing for the Arabs than the immediate control of these weapons. If Israel feels happy and assured with its nuclear capability but is ready to renounce its occupation, there is no harm to its maintaining its current policy in the short term, until the settlement is implemented and tested. Furthermore, effective agreements on controlling these weapons necessitate an intrusive system of inspection and verification with which the parties to the conflict are not as yet ready to tolerate and comply, given the atmosphere of mutual suspicions and acute sense of vulnerability. A possible transitional measure is a declaratory commitment by the would-be members of the regime to no-first-use of these categories of weapons until they are incorporated in the regime. It may well be argued that such a commitment may deprive these weapons of their deterrent value, but it would be a reassuring gesture of psychological import during the implementation of the political settlement.

Missiles

Medium- and long-range ballistic missiles somehow have been connected with weapons of mass destruction as their means of delivery. The Missile Technology Regime of 1987 (MTCR) made this association.[31] It aims at controlling the transfer of technology related to missiles of 300 km range and a payload of 500 kg and above. The grounds on which the distinction is made between these missiles and those with shorter range and less payload are rather arbitrary. Short-range missiles can still carry nuclear and chemical warheads. Moreover, in the geographical context of most regional conflict, including the Arab–Israeli one, short-range missiles can reach many strategic and civilian targets of vital importance. The short-range Lance missile, which Israel possesses, and the SS-21, which is in the Syrian arsenal, are more accurate than the medium-range Jericho-1 and SCUD-B and SCUD-C.

The claim that missiles can more effectively penetrate air-defense systems and are more accurate than fighter-bombers, which can also deliver chemical and nuclear weapons, is very dubious in light of the experience of recent Gulf Wars. Anti-ballistic defense systems, such as the American Patriot and Russian S-300, have been developed and are constantly being improved. Electronic counter-measures (ECM) to suppress air-defense radar have immeasurably enhanced the penetration capability of fighter-bombers as well. Target acquisition technology, such as smart and laser-guided bombs, has made pinpointing intended targets much easier. Military aircraft, with or without aerial refueling, have sufficient radius to hit a great number of strategic targets within the zones of operation of regional conflicts.[32] To impose restrictions on one type of delivery vehicle (missiles) is not really a serious measure of arms control, since the problem is not the missiles themselves but their political-military utility in the context of a certain conflict and their relationship to other delivery systems. Denying the possession of medium-range missiles to developing countries can only be interpreted as a discriminatory measure in favor of developed ones with advanced operational air forces.

Despite the MTCR, Israel, Egypt, Syria, and Iran are pressing ahead with their programs to build up medium-range missile forces, and it is highly unlikely that they will give them up in the near future. Saudi Arabia has also acquired a small force of Chinese C-3 missiles, though they have not been augmented. For the less technologically sophisticated countries, missiles are the appropriate cost-effective response to counter the superiority of air forces operated by advanced states such as Israel. They are cheaper to run and do not require the demanding sophistication needed to operate modern air forces equipped with front-line airplanes. The advantages of missiles are several: they do not need exacting, expensive, and long-term training of pilots and maintenance crews, and there is no need for the continuous flow of spare parts and engine overhauls after a certain number of flying hours, whether for training or military missions. Additionally, the disappearance of the Soviet Union as a reliable supplier for political motives of advanced aircraft on easy credit terms has made the situation even more complicated. Only true Western allies (like Israel) or semi-allies (like Egypt, Saudi Arabia, and Kuwait), can now obtain these systems (whether on credit or for cash), in sufficient quality and quantity. Syria, on the other hand, has now been deprived of the equal opportunity to maintain an efficient air arm. It will be some time before Russia recovers sufficiently economically and industrially in the military field to be able to provide advanced airplanes in large quantities—even in the case of Iran, which is trying to rebuild its air force and has hard currency to spend. under these circumstances, Syria and Iran have no alternative but to veer toward stressing medium-range missiles in their overall mix of military forces so that there is no gap in their defensive capabilities. Attempts to deprive them of a vital element in maintaining military credibility to retaliate if attacked will be vehemently resisted.

There is also an important controversy as to whether or not missiles are inherently destabilizing weapons systems. When they were part of the triad that upheld mutual deterrence during the Cold War, they were regarded as the backbone of stability. In contrast, when Third World states acquired them, they changed their character and became destabilizing. Missiles are not always or in every case destabilizing, as is usually argued.[33] In the Arab–Israeli military environment missiles provide the most efficient path to building a protected second-strike force which considerably reduces the probability of a devastating surprise attack, whether nuclear or conventional, from either side. By posing the threat of retaliation, the defender complicates the calculations of the potential attacker.

Missiles provide all the requirements of a survivable retaliatory force, including mobility, dispersal, concealment, and hardening. The inability of the Allied air forces to pin down and destroy mobile Iraqi missile launchers is a case in point. The survivability of retaliatory forces is also better assured with a sophisticated and integrated air-defense system. When both sides possess survivable retaliatory forces, the stability of mutual deterrence is enhanced rather than decreased. This outcome is strengthened when missiles are designed and targeted with minimal circle of error probabilities (CEP) to avoid collateral damage; that is, as *counter-force weapons.*

It can be argued that counter-value missiles (that is, longer range missiles with larger CEPs) are more stabilizing than more precise counter-force weapons, since the awesome fear of potential civilian casualties and urban havoc would restrain an attacker if damage to an objective was not worth the risk of retaliatory damage to non-military targets caused by a defender's counter-strike. However, in the Arab–Israeli context the balance of the argument favors the more precise counter-*force* missiles, because of the relatively small number of missiles deployed and of the main objectives sought by their deployment.

If the objective is to reduce the likelihood of a surprise attack, then counter-attack targets have to be mainly of a military nature to convince the potential attacker that it would not benefit from a first strike (as its military assets would be subject to a second-strike substantially affecting its ability to continue the war). Second, if the objective is to limit the scope of hostilities in the theater of operation to the battlefield while protecting strategic and civilian targets in the rear, small-CEP counter-force missiles would be more effective in posing a threat to the weapons systems that are capable of hitting these rear targets (i.e., missile launching facilities and airfields from which aircraft operate). This type of threat reinforces the threat of retaliation in kind, namely, to hit cities in exchange for striking cities.

Whatever the relative merits in favor of counter-value or counter-force weapons, it is the availability of a retaliatory strike that, in the final analysis, may dissuade an attacker and influence its calculus more than the type of targets and the degree of damage. Either way, missiles are not so destabilizing to an arms control regime as is often claimed, particularly if the political problems are settled. And if missiles shorten a war and limit its scope and violence, this is still a measure of arms control.

Leaving one side vulnerable and exposed to a devastating surprise attack is certainly not a sound recommendation for encouraging restraint and exercising control in a crisis. It is the feeling of confidence, of not being apprehensive of a comprehensive military defeat, that promotes cold nerves to manage a crisis and bring it to an end with a compromise that satisfies both sides' interests. When one side is vulnerable to a crippling first strike, it would have a strong incentive to take the initiative before it is too late and loses everything politically and militarily.

Obviously, Israel does not like to lose the superiority of its air force. It also fears an Arab first strike with missiles that may neutralize this superiority and disrupt its mobilization system, as the advantage invariably lies with the first strike. Israel's apprehensions are not fully justified for two reasons: first, the possibility of an Arab first strike only arises if Israel does not withdraw from the occupied territories, which would motivate the Arab side to start a war. But even in this scenario, it is unlikely that Syria, for example, would initiate hostilities with a missile salvo, bearing in mind the devastating Israeli retaliation. Second, for the advantage of a first strike to be realized and maximized, it has to be so overwhelming that it leaves no room for effective retaliation. Without nuclear weapons, such an outcome is very difficult to achieve. If hypothetically the Arab side obtains nuclear capabilities, then the scenario shifts to nuclear deterrence.

Missiles, like nuclear and chemical weapons, are not easily subject to control. Control would take a completely different security environment from the one prevailing now between Israeli and the Arab parties. It may come at an advanced stage in building the regime. If, in the meantime, the number, payload and range of missiles can be limited, it would be a helpful step. But in view of Israel's fears regarding Iran and Pakistan, it is doubtful that Israel is open to discussion on such measures. In addition, the monitoring of measures related to missiles would, like nuclear and chemical weapons, face the problems regarding intrusiveness and openness. However, as part of CSBMs, and following Israel's commitment to withdraw, it is feasible to give prior notice of missile testing.

INDIGENOUS MILITARY INDUSTRY

Israel stands out among the states in the Middle East region as having the most developed military industry.[34] However, it has not yet achieved the stage of complete self-sufficiency in all weapons systems, either in quantity or quality. It still relies on American and Western European help, particularly in research and development. The U.S.–Israeli strategic understanding of 1981 covers military cooperation in various areas of research and manufacturing. Added to this edge against the Arab side, the Soviet Union, which was the main backer of Syria and Iraq, has disappeared as a superpower. Hence, the relative importance of indigenous military industry has disproportionately increased in favor of Israel. Although Egypt and Iraq can produce certain items or assemble them,[35] this is a far cry from the sophistication of Israel's military products.

The central problem in subjecting indigenous production of armaments to international inspection not only concerns revealing military secrets, which requires openness, but also protecting commercial and industrial secrets. The best that can be done, within the framework of an arms control regime, is to concentrate on keeping a registry to count the final products delivered to the armed forces of the members. Clearly, this measure has to be adopted in case ceilings are imposed on the main platforms, i.e., tanks, airplanes, armored personnel carriers, heavy guns, and naval craft.

THE VERIFICATION SYSTEM

The experience of Iraq, which managed to circumvent the inspection performed by the IAEA, has vindicated the skeptics of the efficacy of international agencies. Verification is not a simple matter when the parties involved have been fighting each other for decades. If they do not have confidence in the U.N.

agencies, it does not follow that they would accept national inspectors as easily as is assumed.

There is no problem in policing the security arrangements along the borders, since most of the inspection will be done jointly under the supervision of U.N. personnel. The serious problem arises if agreements are reached on limiting or banning several categories of weapons systems, whether conventional or unconventional, requiring inspection inside the territories of the members. Such agreements presuppose a degree of intrusiveness that will not be available except in an advanced stage of political relaxation.[36]

It is therefore suggested that such thorny issues be left until the later phases of establishing the regime. What is essential at the start is to create the prerequisites of a stable strategic environment. This can be done only by the parties themselves through mutual reassurance of true intentions and in response to their respective needs. Mutual inspection would then progress gradually, as the participants come to perceive it to be in their own self-interest to preserve the regime.

Technical means of monitoring and gathering intelligence have, in some areas, obviated the need to perform on-site inspections.[37] Technical means such as aerial reconnaissance and satellite photography may be enough to monitor the locations of airfields, naval bases, and deployment of major armored units. Nevertheless, territorial on-site inspection is still required in the case of nuclear, chemical, biological and missile facilities. The U.N. specialized agencies could be joined by national inspectors which have the authority to demand surprise visits.

An effective verification system must provide for prompt remedy in case of violation. The U.N. Security Council should be empowered to immediately seize on any major violation and act accordingly. Minor violations due to disputes over the interpretation of certain provisions could be dealt with locally by the various joint committees under the chairmanship of U.N. personnel. As for the guarantees offered by the nuclear powers under the NPT, they should be made imperative and generalized to allow the U.N. Security Council to take immediate measures to protect any state exposed to nuclear, chemical and biological threats.

Arms Transfers

It stands to reason that an effective arms control regime requires the cooperation of the external powers. Their behavior will be crucial both politically and strategically, especially in the area of supplying military hardware.[38] President Bush's proposals underscored this fact and called upon the permanent members of the U.N. Security Council to begin formulating a regime to coordinate their activities in this field. It is too early to predict whether the P-5 talks will be a success or failure. So far they have not reached any substantive agreement, and it would be overoptimistic to expect quick results.

The prime reason for this is that policies of arms transfers are subject to a complex process in which several internal and external factors should be balanced.[39] Four interrelated factors can be delineated whose interplay determines the efficacy of a regime to regulate arms supplies:

- the political relationship between the supplier and the recipient;

- the economic and financial rewards involved in selling armaments;

- the strategic interests of the supplier in the entire region in question; and

- the security needs of the client, and how these can be accurately evaluated by the principal supplier.

Each factor influences the willingness of suppliers to provide weapons and the desire of recipients to obtain them.

It is, however, easier to define the problem than to suggest a solution that reconciles all these conflicting variables in every military aid relationship. Moreover, the values assigned to these factors are liable to change over time and according to circumstances. Political attitudes toward a ruling regime in a recipient state may be modified depending on the priorities of the supplier and its perception of whether the former's behavior serves the interest of the supplier. Economic pressures for increased arms sales may also override any political restraint. And if strategic interests are wrongly perceived and reinforced by financial motives, the result can be disastrous, as in the case of Iraq before the second Gulf War.

The problem of limiting external supply of arms has become more complicated with the appearance of a second category of suppliers such as Israel, Brazil, Argentina, South Africa, India and North Korea. With the disintegration of the Soviet Union and its hold over Eastern Europe, a huge surplus of military equipment has also become available on the market. The main incentive for these suppliers is to seek lucrative contracts that earn hard currency. They may not offer front-line items and meet all the needs of buyers, but they make it simpler and quicker to acquire large quantities of hardware, since no political strings are attached.

Consequently, to rely only on the policy of restraint and control, which could be expected from the P-5 talks, is not enough.[40] It may be useful if the regimes on nuclear, chemical, and biological weapons are strictly adhered to. But it would be more helpful if the local parties to the arms control regime themselves exercise the required restraint by capping the arms race until a comprehensive regime is in place. In this respect, since the Arab side has lost its main backer, i.e., the Soviet Union, Israel and the U.S. have to revise the Strategic understanding of 1981, which allows Israel to store American equipment and grants it preferential treatment.

Last, the idea of having a U.N. weapons transfer registry will not work for the simple reason that it would require an ideal world free from conflict and wars. Rightly or wrongly, states consider their military strengths as guarded secrets. The supplier does not want to lose the deal, nor is the recipient interested in revealing all its secrets. When the local parties to an arms control regime agree to restrictions and devise a system of verification it is quite sufficient to monitor the level of armaments which each member holds.

CONCLUSION

It is clear from the previous discussion that the problems cannot be underestimated. Besides the Arab–Israeli conflict, the Middle East as a whole is pregnant with disputes, both open and latent, that might evolve into conflicts and armed hostilities. Grand designs that promise an era of cooperation in the region without first tackling the political agenda are divorced from reality. For any regime of arms control to function properly, there must be a rudimentary concept of common interests. These interests cannot be created as long as the regional protagonists have not settled the political issues that divide them. Therefore, the immediate task at hand is to concentrate on the simmering Arab–Israeli conflict.

Appearances are deceptive if one tends to read too much into the demise of the Cold War and the outcome of the second Gulf War and thus concludes that peace in the Middle East is just around the corner. The international system is in a state of flux and many conditions are ephemeral parameters. The radical change in the primary international system does not lead inevitably to regional order. Quite the reverse: the regional powers will rival each other in order to establish the order that suits their own interests. In this process, given the lack of external restraints resulting from the previous central strategic balance, conflicts and armed hostilities are not necessarily minimized or controlled.

The current multilateral talks on arms control are helpful and could contribute to a political culture basic to building the essential institutional structure or structures that are needed for assuring security and stability. However, three major regional states—Syria, Iraq, and Iran—are so far not taking part in the negotiations. While it is not very urgent to bring in the last two, no regional arms control regime in the Arab–Israeli conflict will function without Syria, which has hinged its participation on progress in the bilateral talks with Israel. Presumably, this progress means that Israel should accept the principle of full withdrawal from the occupied territories. Whether Israel will pronounce this commitment in the near future remains to be seen. Syria has also insisted that any limitation on arms ought to take place within the objective condition of peace, and if arms control measures are to be applied before peace exists, then they will be discussed on the basis of comprehensiveness, justness, equality, and reciprocity for all sides.[41]

In recognition of the complexity of the issues, the need for gradualism, and the importance of having an outline or road map, the envisaged arms control regime outlined above could be implemented in the following phases:

- Phase One: This phase begins with exchanging mutual political commitments on the shape of settlement and the introduction of some CSBMs.

- Phase Two: As the implementation of political agreements proceeds, more CSBMs are applied. Simultaneously, talks on constructing the arms control regime commence.

- Phase Three: When full Israeli withdrawal is achieved and the Palestinians establish their state, the arms control regime is put in place. However, this phase excludes nuclear weapons, chemical weapons and missiles except certain initial measures to control their production or quantities. Obviously, this assumes that Israel will declare itself as a nuclear power and join the NPT.

- Phase Four: Depending on international and regional developments and whether there is an international regime to effectively control nuclear proliferation, the parties to the regime make their own arrangements to destroy their nuclear and chemical weapons stockpiles. They also make drastic cuts in their missile and air forces. This phase could transform the arms control regime into a full "security regime," which assumes a higher degree of political and military cooperation. CSBMs on the ground could be also dismantled in this stage as the members have to all intents and purposes formed regional common interests and no longer fear each other.

The guiding rules for construction of the regime and its implementation ought to be prudence and common sense. In the long run, side stepping or overlooking the harsh realities of deep-seated antagonism will not help the cause of stability and peace.

NOTES

This chapter was prepared as part of a project financed by the United States Institute of Peace, Washington, DC

1. *The Arab–Israeli Peace Process Briefing Book* (Washington, DC: The Washington Institute for Near East Policy, 1991) doc. 2.1 and Doc. 9.22, respectively.

2. Thomas C. Schelling and Morton H. Halperin, *Strategy and Arms Control* (Washington, D. C.: Pergamon-Brassey's Classic, 1985); and Lawrence Freedman, *Arms Control: Management or Reform?*

Chatham House Papers, p. 31 (London: Routledge & Kegan Paul, 1986).

3. William W. Kaufman, "The Requirements of Deterrence," in Philip Bobbitt, Lawrence Freedman, and Gregory F. Treverton, eds., *US Nuclear Strategy: A Reader* (London: Macmillan, 1989) and Thomas Schelling, *Arms and Influence* (New Haven: Yale University Press, 1986).

4. Robert Jervis, Richard Ned Lebow and Janice Gross Stein, *Psychology and Deterrence* (Baltimore: Johns Hopkins University Press, 1985); and Richard Ned Lebow and Janice Gross Stein, "Beyond Deterrence," *Journal of Social Issues,* 42:4 (1987), pp. 5–40.

5. Richard Ned Lebow and Janice Gross Stein, pp. 40–71; and Janice Gross Stein, "Deterrence and Reassurance," in *Behavior, Society and Nuclear Weapons* Vol. 2 (New York: Oxford University Press, 1991), ch. 1.

6. With a few exceptions, there will be no recommendation of specific measures for each side, for two reasons: First, actual data on military capabilities are most guarded secrets, and relying on published materials is not realistic; second, these capabilities are changeable over time and according to political circumstances. The discussion will be confined to prescribing basic guidelines on the issues to be negotiated among the participants in the regime.

7. John Jorgen Holst and Karen Alette Melander, "European Security and Confidence-Building Measures," *Survival,* 19:4 (July/Aug., 1977), 146–54; Jonathan Alford, ed., *The Future of Arms Control: Part III, Confidence-Building Measures*, Adelphi Papers, No. 149 (London: The International Institute for Strategic Studies, 1979); and John Borawski, *From the Atlantic to the Urals: Negotiating Arms Control at the Stockholm Conference* (Washington, DC: Pergamon-Brassey's International Defense Publisher, 1988), chs. 1 and 6.

8. Alan Platt, ed., *Arms Control and Confidence Building in the Middle East* (Washington, DC: United States Institute of Peace Press, 1992).

9. See also David B. Dewitt, "Confidence-and Security-Building Measures in the Middle East: Is There a Role?" in *Conflict Management in the Middle East,* Gabriel Ben-Dor and David B. Dewitt, eds. (Lexington, MA: Lexington Books, 1987), ch. 12.

10. It should be observed that some of these measures have been part of the political culture in the Arab–Israeli conflict since the Armistice Agreements of 1949. Others were also applied between Egypt and Israel after the 1956 war. However, they all failed to prevent the 1967 war. Following the 1973 war, Egypt and Israel gradually developed more extensive measures in 1975, and a limited regime to police the Peace Treaty of 1979, whereas Syria and Israel are still adhering to the measures set forth in the Disengagement Agreement of 1974. As for Lebanon, after the 1978 Israeli invasion a U.N. force has been deployed but it is ineffectual in preventing border incidents. Jordan and Israel still theoretically apply the Armistice Agreement of 1949 pending signing of the new peace agreement. See Yair Evron, *The Role of Arms Control in the Middle East,* Adelphi Papers, No. 138 (London: IISS, 1977).

11. John Mackinlay, *The Peacekeepers: An Assessment of the Peacekeeping Operations at the Arab–Israeli Interface* (London: unwin Hayman, 1989).

12. The idea was originally suggested by Yair Evron, of Tel Aviv University. However, he does not put the U.N. in charge, which makes it difficult for the Arabs to accept, especially in the Israeli withdrawal stage. I disagree with his contention that it is possible to have CSBMs before Israel's commitment to full withdrawal. He also stretches the concept of CSBMs to include any tacit strategic dialogue that is the result of the correlation of forces at a certain time and are not inherently measures of confidence-building with a cumulative effect. See his "Confidence-Building in the Middle East," in Dore Gold, ed., *Arms Control in the Middle East* (Boulder: Westview Press, 1990).

13. John G. Keliher, *The Negotiations on Mutual and Balanced Force Reductions: The Search for Arms Control in Central Europe* (New York: Pergamon Press; n.d.); and Uwe Nerlich and James A.

Thomson, eds., *Conventional Arms Control and the Security of Europe* (Boulder: Westview Press, 1988).

14. Mordechai Gur, "Destabilizing Elements of the Middle East Military Balance," in *Arms Control in the Middle East*, ed. by Dore Gold, op. cit., ch.1.

15. Richard A. Gabriel, ed., *Fighting Armies in the Middle East: A Combat Assessment* (Westport, CT: Greenwood Press, 1983); and Anthony H. Cordesman, *The Arab–Israeli Military Balance and the Art of Operations* (Lanham, MD: University Press of America, 1987).

16. Samuel P. Huntington, "Arms Races: Prerequisites and Results," in *The Use of Force: International Politics and Foreign Policy* (2nd ed., Lanham, MD: University Press of America, 1983), pp. 439–72.

17. Colin S. Gray, "Arms Races and Their Influence upon International Stability, with Special Reference to the Middle East," in *Dynamics of a Conflict: A Re-Examination of the Arab–Israeli Conflict*, Gabriel Sheffer, ed. (Atlantic Highlands, N.J.: Humanities Press, 1975), pp. 39–93; and Yair Evron, Arms Races in the Middle East and Some Arms Control Measures Related to Them," *Ibid.*, pp. 95–135.

18. Saadia Ameil, "Deterrence by Conventional Forces," *Survival*, 20:2 (March/April, 1978), 58–62; Richard K. Betts, *Surprise Attack* (Washington, DC: The Brookings Institution, 1982), pp. 111–14; and Jack S. Levy, "The Offensive/Defensive Balance of Military Technology: A Theoretical and Historical Analysis," *International Studies Quarterly*, 28:2 (1984), 219–38.

19. General A. Merglen, "Military Lessons of the October War," in *The Middle East and the International System: I. The Impact of the 1973 War*, Adelphi papers, No. 114 (London: IISS, 1975), pp. 26–30; and Michael Handel, "Crisis and Surprise in Three Arab–Israeli Wars," with a few exceptions, in *Strategic Military Surprise: Incentives and Opportunities*, Klaus Knorr and Patrick Morgan, eds. (New Brunswick, NJ: Transaction Books, 1983), ch. 5.

20. W. Seth Carus, "Military Lessons of the 1982 Israeli–Syrian Conflict," in *The Lessons of Recent Wars in the Third World: Approaches and Case Studies*, Vol. 1, Robert E. Harkavey and Stephen G. Neuman, eds. (Lexington, MA: Lexington Books, 1985), ch. 12.

21. M. Z. Diab, "Syria's Objectives and Its Concepts of Deterrence, Defense and Security," in *Regional Security in the Middle East: Arab and Israeli Concept of Deterrence and Defense*, David Wurmser, ed. (Washington, DC: United States Institute of Peace, forthcoming).

22. Louis Williams, ed., *Military Aspects of the Israeli–Arab Conflict* (Tel Aviv: University Publishing Projects, 1975), pp. 225–65; U.S. Department of Defense, *Conduct of the Persian Gulf War: Final Report to Congress*, Appendix T (April, 1992).

23. Ariel Levite, *Offense and Defense in Israeli Military Doctrine* (Boulder: Westview Press, 1989), ch. 2; and Dan Horowitz, "The Israeli Concept of National Security and the Prospects of Peace in the Middle East," in *Dynamics of a Conflict*, op. cit., pp. 235–75.

24. John J. Mearsheimer, *Conventional Deterrence* (Ithaca, NY: Cornell University Press, 1983), ch. 5.

25. Alex Gliksman, "Defensive Defense in the Middle East," in *Nonoffensive Defense: A Global Perspective*, UNIDIR (New York: Taylor & Francis, 1990), ch. 8; and Carl Conetta, Charles Knight, and Lutz Unterseher, "Toward Defensive Restructuring in the Middle East," *Bulletin of Peace Proposals*, 22:2 (June, 1991), 115–34.

26. Anthony H. Cordesman, *Weapons of Mass Destruction in the Middle East* (London: Brassey's UK, 1991).

27. Louis Renes Beres, ed., *Security or Armageddon: Israel's Nuclear Strategy* (Lexington, MA: Lexington Books, 1986); Frank Barnaby, *The Invisible Bomb: The Nuclear Arms Race in the Middle East* (London: I.B. Tauris & Co. Ltd., 1989), chs. 2–4; and Honore M. Catudal, Jr., *Israel's Nuclear Weaponry: A New Arms Race in the Middle East* (London: Grey Seal, 1991).

28. Peter Herby, *The Chemical Weapons Convention and Arms Control in the Middle East* (Oslo: PRIO, 1992).

29. For an opposite view see Mahmoud Karem, *A Nuclear-Weapon-Free Zone in the Middle East: Problems and Prospects* (Westport, CT: Greenwood Press, 1988).

30. Nicholas A. Sims, *The Diplomacy of Biological Disarmament: Vicissitudes of Treaty in Force, 1975–85* (London: Macmillan Press, 1988); and Charles C. Flowerre, "Verification of Chemical and Biological Weapons: Lessons Learned," in *Verification: The Key to Arms Control in the 1990s*, John G. Tower, James Brown, and William K. Cheek, eds. (Washington, DC: Brassey's US, Inc., 1992), ch.13.

31. Janne E. Nolan, *Trappings of Power: Ballistics Missiles in the Third World* (Washington, DC: The Brookings Institution, 1993), ch. 2.

32. See *Assessing Ballistic Missile Proliferation and Its Control*, A Report of the Center for International Security and Arms Control, Stanford University, November, 1991.

33. Ibid.; Anthony Cordesman, *Weapons of Mass Destruction in the Middle East*, op. cit.; and W. Seth Carus, *Ballistic Missiles in the Modern Conflict* (New York: Praeger, 1991).

34. Aaron S. Klieman, *Israel's Global Reach: Arms Sales as Diplomacy* (Washington, DC: Pergamon-Brassey's, 1985), ch. 5; and Aharon Klieman and Reuven Pedatzur, *Rearming Israel: Defense Procurement Through the 1990s* (Boulder: Westview Press, 1991).

35. Yezid Sayigh, *Arab Military Industry: Capability, Performance and Impact* (London: Brassey's UK, 1992).

36. Lynn Marvin Hansen, "Verification of Conventional, Missile and Chemical Weapons Agreements," in *Arms Control in the Middle East*, Dore Gold, ed., op. cit., ch. 6.

37. Kosta Tsipis, David W. Hafemeister, and Penny Janeway, eds., *Arms Control Verification: The Technologies That Make It Possible* (Washington, DC: Pergamon-Brassey's, 1986).

38. Ian Smart, "Untangling the Priorities, Weapons, Vehicles, and the Objectives of Arms Control," and Andrei V. Shoumikhin, "Soviet Policy Toward Arms Transfers to the Middle East," in *Arms Control and Weapons Proliferation in the Middle East and South Asia*, Shelley A. Stahl and Geoffrey Kemp, eds. (New York: St. Martin's Press, 1992), chs. 12 and 17, respectively; and Geoffrey Kemp, *The Control of the Middle East Arms Race* (Washington, DC: Carnegie Endowment for International Peace, 1991), ch. 7.

39. Geoffrey Kemp, Ibid., ch. 3; Stephanie G. Neuman, *Military Assistance in Recent Wars: The Dominance of the Superpowers* (New York: Praeger, 1986); and Michael Brzoska and Thomas Ohlson, *Arms Transfers to the Third World, 1971–85* (Oxford: Oxford University Press, 1987), ch. 4.

40. Consider the fate of the Tripartite Declaration of 1950, issued by the U.S., Britain and France. See Michael B. Oren, "The Tripartite System and Arms Control in the Middle East, 1950–1956," in Dore Gold, ed., *Arms Control in the Middle East*. op. cit.

41. President Hafez Al-Assad's speech on March 8, 1993, *Al-Thawra* (Damascus), March 9, 1992, 1–5.

7   Conflicting Approaches to Arms Control in the Middle East: Finding a Common Ground

Gerald M. Steinberg

OVERVIEW

Arms control and confidence-building are central elements in the Arab–Israeli peace process and are the subject of discussions in the multilateral working group on regional security and arms control. Limitation proposals are discussed in numerous other contexts, both at the bilateral level, involving Israel and the individual Arab states (specifically Egypt and Jordan), and in international organizations, including the United Nations and the International Atomic Energy Agency.

In every format and forum, the proposals and concepts presented by Israel and the Arab states contrast sharply. While the Arab states, led by Egypt, place priority on the Israeli nuclear capability and seek unconditional Israeli acceptance of the Nuclear Non-Proliferation Treaty, Israel sees this as the last step in the peace process. Despite progress in negotiations, after decades of conflict, the Israeli leadership continues to be concerned about the military threat to national existence and views the maintenance of a nuclear capability as a necessary deterrent. Indeed, Arab efforts to force Israel to give up its nuclear option before the implementation of a comprehensive regional peace agreement are interpreted as evidence that "the Arab states wish to retain the option of waging wars against Israel, with nothing to worry about."[1]

Instead, Israel emphasizes confidence- and security-building measures (CSBMs). In a January 1993 speech outlining Israeli policy, Shimon Peres gave priority to measures designed "to build and nurture mutual confidence between states" and "to diminish the levels of suspicion, hostility and conflagration," specifically with respect to crisis management and the prevention of accidental war. Examples include prenotification of large-scale military exercises, the development of crisis management mechanisms and hot-lines, and measures to prevent incidents at sea (particularly in the Red Sea area, where the naval forces of Israel, Egypt, Jordan, and Saudi Arabia are active).

This difference in emphasis is reflected in the contrasting agendas presented by Israel and the Arab states. Israeli policy is based on three factors: 1) the interdependence between arms limitations and the peace process (bilateral and multilateral); 2) maintenance of a deterrent capability against "existential" attacks; and 3) the development of regional verification mechanisms based on mutual inspection (without international organizations as intermediaries).

Following the implementation of CSBMs, the Israelis envision agreements on conventional arms limitations, and implementation of the Chemical Weapons Convention by all states (including the development of a framework for mutual verification and inspection). Restraints on strategic systems, including ballistic missiles and nuclear weapons, are longer term goals, to be implemented after peace has been established and other weapons have been subject to restraint. Accession to the NPT is dependent on the negotiation and implementation of a regional nuclear weapon free zone, including mutual inspection and broad verification systems far beyond the existing regime. unilateral concessions in the nuclear realm are rejected.

The Arab position, as embodied in the April 1990 Mubarak Plan and repeated frequently since, is broadly the reverse of the Israeli program. The Egyptian position seeks Israeli acceptance of the NPT as a first step, before other states, such as Iraq or Algeria, are able to develop an advanced nuclear infrastructure. In the attempt to increase pressure on Israel, Egypt has also stressed this issue in connection with its position on the 1995 NPT Review Conference. Although Egyptian policy makers have acknowledged a role for CBMs as well as limitations on conventional weapons, these are placed within the context of an overall peace process and only *after* Israel has signed and implemented the NPT.

Other key Arab countries have backed the Egyptian position, while keeping their distance from the substance of arms controls. Syria is refusing to participate in the multilateral negotiations, including the working group on regional security and arms control, and Saudi Arabia has been a silent observer. Iran, whose participation is essential, has condemned the entire peace process, including arms control negotiations, while acquiring major arsenals of conventional and non-conventional weapons. In contrast to other issues on the agenda of the multilateral talks, such as economic cooperation, water, the environment, and even refugees, progress in arms control and regional security requires the full participation of the major actors, including Syria, Iraq, Iran, and, in some areas, Libya. until these states are involved in the process, the best that can be expected are some limited CSBMs and the creation of a technical and political foundation for verification of future agreements. Substantive limits on missiles and non-conventional weapons are impossible without these key actors.

Efforts to force Israel to accept limitations on its nuclear program in the absence of major political and military changes

in the region are "non-starters." There is little chance that Israel
will change its position prior to the negotiation and
implementation of formal peace treaties with all the major
regional powers, including Iran, Iraq, and perhaps even Libya.
The Arab emphasis on this issue, without reference to Israeli
fears and war scenarios, indicates the gap in positions and
agendas.

Encounters between representatives of the major states in the
region demonstrate the wide gap in perceptions and the high
degree of misperceptions that exist. The gulf between Israeli and
Egyptian perceptions is still very wide, despite over 15 years of
direct interaction. Both sides insist that the other enjoys
conventional superiority (the Israelis refer to potential Arab
coalitions). The Arab policy reflects little recognition or
appreciation of the geographic and demographic asymmetries
that effect Israeli security requirements, the impact of the past 45
years of warfare, and the Israeli emphasis on self-reliance. There
is little understanding of the impact of events prior to the 1967
war on Israeli threat perceptions and of the fear that if the peace
process leads to a return to the pre-1967 boundaries, the threat of
a large scale conventional attack will again pose an existential
threat to the state.

Thus, at this preliminary stage, the first objective of the
regional security and arms control process should be to facilitate
communication between the parties, allowing both to understand
the primary factors that motivate the policies and doctrine of the
others. The prime element in this process, which, in itself, is an
essential confidence-building measure, is repeated in
discussions, meetings, and seminars in which these issues are
discussed. The extent of misunderstanding and lack of
knowledge in relations between Israel and the Arabs is
extensive, and a major effort is required to overcome this barrier.
As the U.S.–Soviet experience demonstrated, the
implementation of significant arms control measures is
facilitated by repeated discussion of the threat perceptions,

strategic doctrines, and decision-making processes of all participants.

At the same time, discussion and implementation of CSBMs can begin, while simultaneously defining a package of limitations that can be implemented once the military and political prerequisites exist. To satisfy the stated objectives of both sides, such a package must include all forms of weapons systems (conventional, CBW, missiles, and nuclear weapons) and regional verification and mutual inspection regimes. Progress toward this goal may be slow, but without this approach, no progress is likely at all.

THE ISRAELI APPROACH TO REGIONAL SECURITY AND ARMS CONTROL

Historically, Israeli political and military leaders have viewed efforts to reach arms limitation agreements in the Middle East with great skepticism. Previous efforts, including the Tripartite Declaration of the 1950s, the NPT/IAEA regime, and other conventions are viewed as failures from the Israeli perspective.[2] At best, arms control was seen as an idealistic irrelevance to the Middle East; at worst, it was a means of weakening and isolating Israel, both militarily and politically. The Middle East continues to be highly unstable, and Israel continues to be vulnerable. Israelis fear that a significant reduction in their deterrent would increase the military threat and the probability of a major war in the region. Israel is very small, lacks strategic depth, and there are many potential threats, from Algeria to Iran.

There is a wide consensus regarding the continued need for a nuclear deterrent, both within the political and military leadership and as reflected in public opinion polls. (In 1991, just after the Gulf War and Iraqi threats to "incinerate half of Israel" with chemical weapons, 88% of Israelis agreed that the use of nuclear weapons under certain circumstances was "justified in principle.")[3] Shalheveth Freier, who served as Israel's representative in international arms control discussions and has played a major role in policy making for many years, noted that all of Israel's major wars resulted from challenges to the existence of Israel. He describes the nuclear deterrent as providing "a sense of reassurance to Israelis in times of gloom" and a "caution to states contemplating obliterating Israel by dint of their preponderance of men and material."[4]

In recent years, policy makers have begun to examine and compare the potential impacts of specific proposals with respect to political and military scenarios. The Israeli government has created new institutions for arms control and has developed a policy based on three essential requirements. First, CSBMs and arms control are directly dependent on the peace process. Progress is closely linked to the negotiations, and while CSBMs and conventional arms limits can be agreed upon and implemented in the course of negotiations, major limitations on Israel's strategic nuclear capability are seen as the final step, after all the states in the region explicitly accept the legitimacy of the Jewish state, and formal peace agreements are signed. Second, limitations must provide a tangible reduction in the military threat, conventional and unconventional, to Israel. Third, limitation agreements must include realistic provisions for verification and solutions to the problem of "breakout" (the sudden unilateral abrogation of limitations by one or more parties, in the effort to achieve a major strategic advantage). Each factor is seen as a necessary and independent requirement for arms control in the region.

ARMS CONTROL, CSBMS, AND THE PEACE PROCESS

Israeli national security and arms control policies are based on a realist approach to the use of force and threat perception. Israeli emphasis on deterrence was formed in response to Arab rejection of the concept of a Jewish state and with full cognizance of the narrow borders and absence of strategic depth. The combined invasions of 1948 (which seriously threatened the survival of the new state); the Egyptian, Syrian, Jordanian, and Iraqi preparations for attack in 1967, and threats to "slice Israel in two," plus the very costly surprise attack in 1973 all contributed to Israeli strategic culture and policies.

Thus, from the Israeli perspective, serious arms control agreements involving limits on the Israeli deterrent can only be implemented when all of these states accept Israel's legitimacy, without reservation, end the state of war, and no longer possess the capability to mount an "existential" attack.[5] Ambiguous and reversible measures are insufficient to allay these deeply imbedded security concerns. After decades of bitter ethnonational and religious violence and warfare, Israel will continue to view the Arab and Islamic worlds with great caution. Before significant limits on its nuclear and missile deterrents are accepted, Israeli policy makers require the removal of the threat from all the Islamic states, including Iraq, Libya, Iran and Algeria.[6] For this reason, direct negotiations, formal peace treaties, and normalization with all the states in the region are necessary pre-conditions for arms control in the region.[7]

This does not mean, however, that nothing can be done about arms control until this stage has been reached. Indeed, in order to make progress in this direction and until the conditions exist to deal with strategic systems and nuclear weapons, CSBMs can play an important role. In the U.S.–Soviet and CSCE arms control processes, the development of small scale and incremental CSBMs provided an indispensable foundation for progress toward more extensive agreements on strategic systems. Such measures, by definition, do not involve significant risks to national security or deterrence and do not require extensive verification or inspection with all the complications that are included in these processes.

In the Middle East, with its history of conflict and the absence of cooperation, CSBMs are clearly necessary to create the conditions for negotiations of arms limitations. For the Israeli government, this phase is critical, as reflected in Foreign Minister Peres's January 1993 speech outlining Israeli policy. Pre-notification agreements regarding large-scale military maneuvers as well as regular communications between military commanders and crisis management measures are considered to be primary areas for CSBMs.

For Israel, the degree of cooperation and direct, frequent and visible contact with the Arab states is critical; unilateral measures will not build confidence that the era in which the Arab states threatened Israel with extinction has finally and irrevocably ended. Ariel Levite, a member of the Israeli delegation in the working group, has noted that CSBMs are "a symbol of cooperation, sending a broad political message of willingness to move beyond confrontation and competition to cooperation and reconciliation."[8]

ARMS CONTROL AND ISRAELI DETERRENCE

The Israeli nuclear deterrent and missile delivery systems were developed in response to the threat of a large-scale combined conventional attack, similar to the 1948 and 1973 wars, and the threat posed prior to the 1967 war. The peace treaty with Egypt, the disintegration of the Soviet Union, and the 1991 Gulf War, which reduced the Iraqi military capability, have reduced this threat. However, the possibility of an attack on the Eastern front, involving Syria, with potential support from Iraq, Jordan, and Saudi Arabia, remains.[9]   With the limited participation of Iraq and Saudi Arabia, Israel would face a disadvantage of 1:2 in tanks, 1:3 in guns and artillery, and 1:2 in combat aircraft.[10] A surprise attack before Israel could mobilize its reserves would greatly increase the Arab advantage.[11] In addition, advanced weapons technology sold to Saudi Arabia and Egypt diffuses quickly throughout the Arab world, leading to an erosion of Israel's technological advantage which has been used to offset the quantitative advantage of the Arabs.[12] Thus, limits of conventional weapons are seen as a prerequisite for restraints on nuclear weapons and long-range surface-to-surface missiles.[13]

Furthermore, any peace agreements that involve territorial withdrawal on the Golan Heights and West Bank could increase the dangers of military attack, requiring expanded Israeli deterrence and defensive capabilities.[14] The geographic and demographic asymmetries that have characterized the Arab–Israeli conflict will become even more pronounced. Israel will always be a micro-state without strategic depth or a large population. If there are changes in the defense lines, Israel will again appear to be highly vulnerable to large-scale surprise attack. Thus, even with peace treaties, arms limitations measures must allow Israel to maintain sufficient military capability to deter and defend against attacks that threaten national survival. As long as the Arab forces maintain significant advantages in conventional forces, the need for a strategic deterrent will continue.

THE PROBLEMS OF COMPLIANCE AND BREAKOUT

Verification of compliance is essential to any realistic arms control regime, and the Middle East has a poor track record in this area. With a few exceptions (such as Israel), most Middle Eastern societies are tightly sealed, making it easy to hide illicit programs and making verification particularly difficult, as was seen in the case of Iraq. The Iraqi regime blatantly violated the 1925 Geneva Convention banning the use of chemical weapons and ignored its commitments under the NPT. In Iraq, IAEA inspections and safeguards were a travesty, and even after the 1991 war, the IAEA was blocked in its efforts to destroy the Iraqi program. (The IAEA employs only 200 inspectors, and most of their time is spent on inspections in countries such as Canada and Sweden.) As long as this situation continues, and there is no way to insure "timely warning" of a nuclear program, such loose international regimes that present the illusion, but not the substance, of verification will be rejected by Israel.

Politically, the IAEA and NPT regime was and still is used for "Israel bashing," and Israel has no trust in such international organizations. For many years, the Arab states have introduced resolutions seeking to expel Israel from the IAEA.[15] Although relations and cooperation have improved, Israel continues to view the IAEA with caution and will not transfer vital national security functions to this organization. Instead, when nuclear arms control is finally on the agenda, Israeli participation is predicated on a regional framework in the form of a Middle East Nuclear Weapon Free Zone (MENWFZ).[16] Based on the model provided by the Treaty of Tlatelolco, such a framework would be negotiated directly between all the states, and verification would be conducted through mutual inspection. This would require the creation of a new and independent regional organization, similar to OPANAL, which was established for the Latin American nuclear free zone. The MENWFZ would include Israeli inspectors in Syria, Iran, and Iraq, and, of course, the reverse.[17]

The Chemical Weapons Convention provides a framework for the establishment of a regional inspection system. Indeed, Israeli policy sees the CWC as a model for the implementation of a nuclear-weapon-free zone (NWFZ).[18] If the negotiation and implementation of verification procedures for the CWC in the region are successful from the Israeli perspective, insuring that the signatories are abiding by the agreement, while non-signatories are denied materials and facilities for the acquisition of chemical weapons, Israel will be able to apply this experience to the development of a NWFZ in the region. As will be discussed in detail below, the IAEA's nuclear verification system is considered by Israel to be inadequate, and Israel is excluded from the IAEA's governing agencies and institutions. Israeli policy emphasizes full participation in the structure of the CWC and the development of adequate verification systems. If this position is accepted with respect to the CWC, some major obstacles to participation in a Middle East NWFZ will be ameliorated.

Thus, the Israeli policy is based on a progression from CSBMs and conventional arms limitations to the establishment of regional limitations on chemical weapons and, finally, a similar framework for a MENWFZ. Each step is linked to and dependent on successful implementation of the previous measure, and efforts to skip stages and move to limitations on the Israeli nuclear program will be strongly resisted.

ARAB VIEWS ON ARMS CONTROL

Egypt signed the NPT in 1981, and since then, has sought to pressure Israel into following this lead. Egyptian leaders argue repeatedly that the nuclear monopoly provides Israel with military superiority that the Arabs, in general, and Egypt, in particular, cannot accept. In addition, from the Egyptian perspective, the Israeli nuclear program makes it difficult to block the nuclear programs of other states in the region, including Iran and Algeria, and will eventually lead to a nuclear Middle East. unless the Israeli program is curbed, the Egyptians warn that they will not support extension of the NPT in the 1995 Review Conference. Egypt has also refused to sign the CWC, linking this to Israeli acceptance of the NPT.

Since 1974, Egypt has been a primary supporter of United Nations resolutions calling for the establishment of a Middle East Nuclear Weapon Free Zone, in which all the states would ratify the NPT. Mahmoud Karem, a senior member of the Foreign Ministry, has published a book entitled *A Nuclear-Weapon-Free Zone in the Middle East: Problems and Prospects*, that presents the Egyptian perspective.[19] This approach, in contrast to the Israeli view, is based on a global verification framework, including the existing IAEA system, and provides an active role for the United Nations.[20] The Egyptian proposal was developed further in April 1990, following Saddam Hussein's announcement of the development of binary chemical weapons. President Mubarak introduced a plan for the establishment of a Middle East Weapons of Mass Destruction Free Zone, and this proposal has been repeated in the context of the multilateral working group on regional security and arms control and the other frameworks.

The Egyptian position is generally accepted by the other Arab states and the Palestinians. The Jordanian delegation to the bilateral negotiations in Washington insisted that the issue of the Israeli nuclear capability be included in the framework agreement setting the agenda for these talks. Others, such as Yezid Sayigh, who is part of the Palestinian delegation to the multilateral talks, also emphasize the Israeli nuclear capability. (However, Sayigh's analysis is inconsistent. While claiming that the Israeli nuclear option constitutes a major threat to the Arabs, he also discusses the Israeli deterrent posture, presenting a scenario in which it "detonates a single weapon demonstratively, to halt an enemy offensive at an early stage and abort it before it poses a threat to national survival.") [21]

As noted above, the Arab position is that Israel must give up its nuclear capability, or at least take major steps in that direction, before the completion of, or in the context of a peace treaty. [22] How, they ask, can the Arabs be persuaded to make peace as long as Israel has a nuclear monopoly and is also holding occupied territories? Egyptian representatives in the United Nations and other international forums have stated that accession to the NPT and acceptance of IAEA safeguards (as well as unspecified "additional steps") constitute confidence-building measures necessary to facilitate the development of a NWFZ. [23] Thus, Israeli concessions on the nuclear issue are seen as an inducement to bring the other Arab states into the peace process and reduce the isolation of Egypt on this issue.

In formulating this position, the Egyptians have not responded to the Israeli proposals for the creation of an independent regional framework in the context of a NWFZ, similar to the Latin American or Pacific regions, and continue to focus on a prominent role of the United Nations, the NPT, and the IAEA system. Policy statements highlight the need to ensure that "any regional arrangement or measure of disarmament" is consistent with "the purposes and principles enshrined in the Charter of the United Nations" and with "the revitalization of the united Nation's role in the fields of disarmament and international security."[24]

In international organizations, in general, and the United Nations, in particular, their numbers give the Arab states a major advantage. In addition, for Egypt, the role of the U.N. has broader foreign policy implications. Since the 1950s, Egypt has often defined its international role in terms of the United Nations, and was a leader and co-founder of the Non-Aligned Movement. This factor, and the Egyptian interest in maintaining a visible role for the United Nations, adds another complication to the politics of arms control in the region.

Formally, the Arab position, as expressed in the United Nations and other international forums, makes no mention of Israeli concerns or stated requirements.[25] Egyptian policy makers have dismissed Israeli fears of conventional attack, arguing that the 1978 Peace Treaty has removed the primary threat to Israel, and the end of the Cold War and the collapse of the Soviet Union have deprived Syria of the major source of weapons. In addition, Egyptians point out that the defeat of Iraq in the 1991 Gulf War has removed another threat. According to the Arab position, the Israeli technological advantage also provides conventional superiority, and therefore the nuclear deterrent is unnecessary. Although Cairo acknowledges the need for improved IAEA safeguards, Egyptian spokesmen have not responded to the criticism of existing safeguards and inspection systems, which Israel has rejected as unacceptable.

Abstractly, the Egyptians have accepted the requirement for CBMs but have defined these in order to include the Israeli nuclear program within this framework. Nabil Fahmy, who plays an important role in the formulation of policy in the Foreign Ministry, has referred to the Egyptian acceptance of the NPT as a CBM and has called on Israel to follow this lead. (Israel rejects this position, on the grounds that strategic systems are beyond the scope of CBMs, and the NPT and IAEA regime involve complex safeguards that are also, by definition, not included in the CBM stage.) Although a number of CBMs operate in the context of the Peace Treaty, including pre-notification of exercises near the borders, demilitarized as well as reduced forces zones, and direct communications between military officers, the Egyptians have not, as yet, actively supported regional multilateral CBMs, such as the creation of regional crisis centers.

While generally endorsing the Egyptian position on nuclear weapons, Jordan has shown greater interest in CSBMs. The head of the Jordanian delegation to the working group on regional security and arms control, Dr. Abdullah Toukan, has called for the exchange of military information, the development of a crisis communications network, an arms registry (the details of which are left ambiguous), and guidelines (qualitative as well as quantitative) to govern the acquisition of conventional weapons. These are consistent with the Israeli program but are listed in an undifferentiated manner with other measures, including demands for universal adoption of the NPT and IAEA safeguards and a halt to the production of fissile material.[26] Thus, the Jordanian position is somewhat ambiguous, incorporating all the elements that are under discussion.

BREAKING THE DEADLOCK

Despite the conflicting views, there are some substantive measures that can potentially bridge these gaps. A full menu would include expanded "seminars" on the security perceptions and policies of the individual nations, incremental implementation of confidence and security-building measures, limits on conventional arms sales and acquisitions, and development of the technology and framework for regional verification and inspection mechanisms for chemical, biological, and nuclear weapons. At the same time, it is important to identify proposals that are "non-starters" and even counterproductive. In particular, efforts to press Israel to accept unilateral limits on its strategic deterrent (including both missile delivery systems and nuclear activities) are likely to trigger Israeli rejection of the process.

Seminar on Regional Security

The first sessions of the multilateral working group on arms control were devoted to a series of seminars to familiarize the participants with the issues and background, particularly with respect to the U.S.–Soviet and European arms control experience. Seminars are also less likely to lead directly to confrontation and deadlock in comparison to formal negotiations.

As could have been expected, these meetings and discussions, both formal and informal, showed a wide gap in evaluation of each others' military capabilities and threat perceptions. Arms control is clearly inseparable from these issues, and without greater understanding and some agreement on the nature of the threat and the military capabilities of each of the parties, progress toward mutual limitations will be slow or impossible.

Given the differences in threat perceptions, a series of seminars or discussions on these issues would be a useful contribution to the arms control and CSBM process. Such seminars, involving both political leaders and military officers,[27] would give the Israelis an opportunity to present their concerns regarding conventional attacks from combined Arab forces, and would allow the Arabs to present their views of Israeli technological superiority. Although little agreement can be expected, the exchange of views is important.

In addition, at this stage, academics and policy makers from the U.S. and Europe would have the opportunity to introduce concepts such as *worst-case analysis* and the *security dilemma,* and show the role of these factors in understanding the Middle East. By placing the differing concepts in a broader analytic framework, it may be easier to discuss the conflicting views, as well as points of agreement regarding common threats, and to define arms limitation policies and CSBMs that minimize the risks and maximize mutual interests.

Confidence- and Security-Building Measures

As in the case of U.S.–Soviet arms control and the CSCE, confidence- and security-building measures that do not involve significant risks and do not require extensive verification systems can provide a foundation for more ambitious measures. In the opening session of the multilateral working group on regional security and arms control, U.S. Secretary of State James Baker proposed that following the first phase of seminars, the process should move to "considering a set of confidence-building or transparency measures covering notifications of selected military activities and crisis prevention communications."

A number of CSBMs have been proposed, including expansion of those listed above to include other states, and a communications and crisis prevention center, which would include Israel, Egypt, Jordan and Saudi Arabia (and would not require Syrian participation). The proposed seminars on threat perceptions and worst case analyses can also be viewed as a CSBM. In order to increase the rate of progress in these areas, the participants in the May 1993 meeting of the multilateral working group established four subgroups which meet more frequently and develop operative proposals; pre-notification (led by Turkey); communications between military commanders (led by Holland); air and naval search and rescue (led by Canada); and policy declarations regarding non-aggression, surprise attack, etc. In addition, the participating states agreed to site-visits to NATO bases and to observe exercises in order to learn more about the measures adopted in the Conventional Forces in Europe (CFE) system.[28]

Conventional Weapons Limitations

During the Cold War, the U.S. and NATO rejected limits on the deployment of nuclear weapons in Europe as long as the USSR and Warsaw Pact enjoyed a major advantage in conventional forces. Similarly, as noted above, Israel will resist any limits on its nuclear deterrent until the threat posed by conventional weapons in the region is reduced significantly. Conventional weapons limitations, including restraints on both supply and acquisition, are necessary components of regional arms control. To further this process, the establishment of a committee on conventional arms limitations within the framework of the multilateral working group would be useful.

Such a framework could include the major arms purchasers in the region (Egypt, Saudi Arabia, Jordan, Israel, and Turkey), as well as the major conventional arms suppliers (all of the P-5 states and Germany) that are participating in the multilateral negotiations. Although other key states such as Syria and Iran, among the recipients, and North Korea, among the suppliers, are not involved, significant progress in this area can still take place.

This group could consider the various proposals that have been discussed, including a freeze on the transfer of major weapons platforms into the region (combat aircraft, main battle tanks, artillery launchers, etc.);[29] supplier limitations, such as agreed-upon guidelines for arms transfers, formal notification of pending arms sales, and the United Nations arms transfer registry; and lessons from the 1950 Tripartite Agreement (which

Israel views as a failure, because the exceptions for "legitimate self defense" allowed the Arab states to obtain weapons but restricted Israeli access). In addition, issues such as verification and limits on local arms industries (which can upgrade weapons but are not capable of producing new platforms independently) can be included.

Beyond these discussions, the major suppliers, and the United States in particular, are in a position to take unilateral action to give this process a push in the right direction. In the wake of the 1991 Gulf War, the supplier states discussed various means of reducing the flow of conventional arms to the region. This was an integral part of U.S. May 1991 Middle East Arms Control Initiative.

Since then and in the wake of the major arms sales announced during the 1992 Presidential election campaign, these proposals have been ignored. Continued large-scale arms sales to the region have undermined the credibility of the American efforts to promote restraint among other suppliers, as well as among the states in the region. In order to get the process moving, the U.S. should consider major changes in its arms sales policies. The Americans will then be in a position to influence other suppliers, including Russia, France, Britain, and China, and, in the longer term, such restraint could also contribute to regional acceptance of conventional arms limitations.

In addition, changes in conventional force structures, including reduction of standing forces and the adoption of reserve systems in Arab countries, can also be considered in this context. Reserve forces are inherently less threatening; they reduce the threat of surprise attack and their offensive potential is greatly reduced as compared to standing forces.

Regional Verification Technology and Frameworks

As noted above, the Arab position emphasizes the issue of nuclear arms control. Progress in other areas is unlikely without attention to this issue. At the same time, the Israelis reject existing verification mechanisms and the structure of the IAEA as inadequate for the Middle East. In order to make progress on this issue, a comprehensive regional project, including the development of the technology for verification, and the political and organization framework, can be undertaken.

The technological core of this project would be a program for research, development, and training focusing on the verification of limitations of conventional, chemical, biological, and nuclear weapons. The first stage would involve identification of the technologies involved, followed by demonstration and simulation programs involving participation of all the major actors. American and Russian technical experts can participate (in an extension of the seminars that were held in 1992), but it is important that the research and development be guided by the participants from the region. This process would, in itself, be an important form of confidence-building, while the substance would provide the infrastructure for implementation of verification systems in the region.

The political and procedural details for regional verification and inspection can also be examined in this context. Since Israel sees the NPT system, in general, and the IAEA, in particular, as politically biased and technically insufficient, an independent regional framework must be created for this process. Israel has rejected discussions on regional verification that are conducted under the auspices of the IAEA. Mechanisms for challenge inspections, continuous monitoring of specific facilities by multinational teams, and procedures for dealing with disagreements, suspected violations, and "breakout" must also be considered. These activities, conducted within the framework of the multilateral working group, could provide the nucleus for a regional framework.

UNILATERAL RESTRAINTS AT DIMONA: A NON-STARTER

In addition to seeking measures that can accelerate this process, it is also important to identify policies and proposals that can have a negative effect on the negotiations. For example, while there have been a number of proposals that Israel accept unilateral limits on its nuclear activities, (i.e., a cutoff in the production of fissile material), there is little chance that this would be acceptable.

From the Israeli perspective, such proposals are seen as the first steps "down the slippery slope" which will lead, in the longer term, to the end of the strategic deterrent, and thereby revive the basis for large-scale Arab attacks. Instead of responding with limits on their own programs, in response to concessions, Israelis fear that the Arab states will simply demand more limitations, including an end to the Israeli deterrent capability. The acceptance of unilateral moves in this area would undermine the emphasis Israel has placed on the development of reliable and regionally based verification regimes. Any incentives that the Arab states have to participate in direct negotiations on such regional regimes would disappear if Israeli were to take major steps on a unilateral basis.

In addition, regardless of any Israeli moves, Iran and Algeria are seen as likely to continue to pursue nuclear weapons and a "freeze" at Dimona could even spur the efforts of the other states.[30] Thus, external pressures to make concessions on these vital points or to accept ad hoc and unilateral measures that fail to tangibly and visibly contribute to Israeli security are likely to be rejected.

CONCLUSIONS

Arms control and confidence-building are central to any Arab–Israeli peace agreement, but the major asymmetries, imbalances, and wide gaps in perceptions place firm limits on what can be accomplished toward this goal. Prescriptions and recommendations for the multilateral working group on regional security and arms control that do not recognize these realities will fail, and may impede the broader political process. Continued interaction, including the exchange of perceptions and "worst case" scenarios and the implementation of CSBMs that are consistent with these conditions, are important first steps in this process.

This does not mean that more substantive measures cannot be discussed, and in order to reconcile the Egyptian and Israeli positions, discussion of these issues must proceed simultaneously. While holding the regional security seminars and implementing CSBMs, discussions of conventional arms limitations and of Chemical and Biological Weapons (CBW) verification can proceed within committees of the working group.

Finally, it important to recognize that although the U.S. and other outsiders can provide assistance, they should not attempt to control the process. The U.S. can influence the process through example (by visibly restricting the sale of weapons, despite clear political and economic costs), and material contributions in the areas of verification technology development and testing. However, for this process to succeed, the states in the region, and the core states of Egypt, Israel, Jordan, Saudi Arabia (and inevitably Syria, if there is to be progress) must be actively engaged.

NOTES

1. Shalheveth Freier, "A Nuclear-Weapon-Free Zone (NWFZ) in the Middle East and Its Ambience," manuscript unpublished, 1993.

2. Michael B. Oren, "The Tripartite System and Arms Control in the Middle East: 1950–1956," in *Arms Control in the Middle East*, Dore Gold, ed. (Boulder: Westview Press, 1990).

3. Asher Arian, "Israel and the Peace Process: Security and Political Attitudes in 1993," Jaffee Center for Strategic Studies Memorandum No. 39, Tel Aviv University, February, 1993, p. 12

4. Shalheveth Freier, "A Nuclear-Weapon-Free Zone (NWFZ) in the Middle East and Its Ambience," op. cit.

5. Address by the Foreign Minister of Israel, Mr. Shimon Peres at the Signing Ceremony of the Chemical Weapons Convention Treaty, Paris, January 13, 1993; see also Shalheveth Freier, "A Nuclear-Weapon-Free Zone (NWFZ) in the Middle East and its Ambience," op. cit.

6. The centrality of this requirement has been recognized by many American policy makers and analysts. Kemp, for example, states that "until there is a long period of peace in the Middle East, Israel is unlikely to negotiate away its nuclear force . . . Pushing Israel too hard on nuclear weapons while demanding that it be more flexible on giving up land for peace would be counterproductive." Geoffrey Kemp, *The Control of the Middle East Arms Race* (Washington, DC: Carnegie Endowment for International Peace, 1992, p. 180).

7. When missiles and nuclear weapons are considered, Pakistan is generally included in the region as well. See, for example, "Establishment of a Nuclear-Weapon-Free Zone in the Region of the Middle East Study on Effective and Verifiable Measures Which Would Facilitate the Establishment of a Nuclear-Weapon-Free Zone in the Middle East," Report of the Secretary General, United Nations General Assembly, A/45/435, 10 October, 1990.

8. Ariel E. Levite, "Confidence and Security Building Measures in the Middle East," draft of paper presented at the UNIDIR Conference, Cairo, April 18–20, 1993.

9. Michael Eisenstadt, "Arming for Peace? Syria's Elusive Quest for 'Strategic Parity'," The Washington Institute for Near East Policy, Policy Paper No. 31, 1992.

10. Joseph Alpher, Zeev Eytan, and Dov Tamari, eds., *Middle East Military Balance, 1989–1990* (Tel Aviv: Jaffee Center for Strategic Studies, Tel Aviv University, 1991).

11. A worst-case scenario involving full participation of the major confrontation states would leave Israel at a 2.6:1 disadvantage in tanks, 4.6:1 disadvantage in guns and mortars, and 2.2:1 deficit in combat aircraft. See *Middle East Military Balance, 1990–1991* (Tel Aviv: Jaffee Center for Strategic Studies, Tel Aviv University, 1992), pp. 404–5.

12. Dore Gold, "U.S. Policy Toward Israel's Qualitative Edge" Jaffee Center for Strategic Studies, Report No. 36, September, 1992, Tel Aviv University, Tel Aviv.

13. See Shalheveth Freier, "A Nuclear-Weapon-Free Zone (NWFZ) in the Middle East and Its Ambience"; and Address by the Foreign Minister of Israel, Mr. Shimon Peres at the Signing Ceremony of the Chemical Weapons Convention Treaty, Paris, 13 January, 1993.

14. For a detailed analysis of the role of territory in Middle Eastern arms control, see Geoffrey Kemp, *The Control of the Middle East Arms Race* (Washington, DC: Carnegie Endowment, 1992) and Alan Platt, ed., *Arms Control and Confidence Building in the Middle East* (Washington, DC: United States Institute for Peace, 1992).

15. Avi Beker, *Disarmament Without Order: The Politics of Disarmament in the United Nations* (Westport: Greenwood Press, 1985); and Avi Beker, "A Regional Non-Proliferation Treaty for the Middle East," *Security or Armageddon: Israel's Nuclear Strategy*, Louis Rene Beres, ed. (Lexington, MA: Lexington Books, 1985).

16. Support for a MENWFZ can be traced to the 1970s. In 1975, Foreign Minister Yigal Allon expressed this support before the United

Nations General Assembly, while also stating the Israeli position that such a zone must be negotiated directly between all the states and not via the United Nations. See Avi Beker, "A Regional Non-Proliferation Treaty for the Middle East," *Security or Armageddon: Israel's Nuclear Strategy*, Louis Rene Beres, ed. (Lexington, MA, Lexington Books, 1985); and Ran Marom, "Israel's Position on Non-Proliferation" *Jerusalem Journal of International Relations*, 8:4, 1986, 118–123.

17. Address by the Foreign Minister of Israel, Mr. Shimon Peres at the Signing Ceremony of the Chemical Weapons Convention Treaty, Paris, 13 January, 1993.

18. For a detailed analysis of the verification issue, see Patricia Bliss McFate, "Where Do We Go From Here? Verifying Future Arms-Control Agreements," *Washington Quarterly* 15:4 (Autumn, 1992).

19. Mahmoud Karem, *A Nuclear-Weapon-Free Zone in the Middle East: Problems and Prospects* (Westport, CT: Greenwood Press, 1988).

20. Daniel Mustacchi, *Can a Nuclear-Weapon-Free Zone be Established in the Middle East? If So, under What Conditions?* unpublished M.A. Thesis, Department of International Relations, Hebrew University, Jerusalem, September, 1992.

21. Yezid Sayigh, "Reversing the Middle East Nuclear Race" *Middle East Report*, No. 177, 22: 4 (July–August, 1992), 1617.

22. Some analysts have suggested that Egypt and other Arab states will accept a unilateral freeze on Israeli nuclear capabilities, in order to prevent the development of a nuclear Middle East, including Iran, Iraq, and Libya. See, for example, Avner Cohen and Marvin Miller, "How to Think About–and Implement–Nuclear Arms Control in the Middle East," *The Washington Quarterly,* Spring, 1993, 101–113. The available evidence, however, does not support this conjecture. While Egypt can be expected to welcome unilateral limits on the Israeli nuclear program, this is not likely to be sufficient to meet Cairo's objectives.

23. *Establishment of a Nuclear-Weapon-Free Zone in the Region of the Middle East,* Report of the Secretary General, Replies Received

from Governments United Nations General Assembly, A/46/291, 25 July, 1991 (cited by Mustacchi).

24. Statement by Dr. Mounir Zaharan, Permanent Representative of Egypt to the United Nations Office and Other International Organizations in Geneva on Regional Disarmament, before the UNIDIR Regional Conference of Research Institutes in the Middle East, Cairo, April 18, 1993, 1, 6.

25. See Mustacchi, passim.

26. Abdullah Toukan, "Strengthening and Creation of Institutional Mechanisms for Middle Eastern Security and Disarmament" presented at the UNIDIR Conference on Research Institutes in the Middle East, Cairo, April 18–19, 1993.

27. In any arms control discussions, it is important to involve the military at an early stage. Throughout the history of U.S.–Soviet negotiations, military officers on both sides opposed limitations agreements, and in most cases, progress was only possible after the military provided its support. In most countries of the Middle East, the military has the power to block any agreement, and many years of effort will be required to obtain the cooperation of senior officers.

28. CSBMs might also be developed on the basis of informal actions which would invite reciprocal response from the other states. For example, Israel has decided not to purchase AMRAM radar guided missiles from the U.S., in the hope that other states (both suppliers and recipients) would also exercise restraint. unilateral moves by Saudi Arabia with respect to arms acquisitions, or by Syria with respect to the size of its standing army and deployments near the border with Israel, could also be considered in this context. Because these CSBMs are informal and do not require detailed negotiations, they may be easier to implement in comparison to formal agreements. However, the scope of informal CBMs is limited to relatively minor areas. For an analysis of a similar process in the U.S.–Soviet context, see Gerald M. Steinberg, *Satellite Reconnaissance: The Role of Informal Bargaining* (New York: Praeger, 1983).

29. See Gerald M. Steinberg, "Opportunities for Conventional Arms Limitations in the Middle East and Persian Gulf," in Andrew Pierre, ed., *Conventional Arms Sales in the 1990s*, forthcoming.

30.   Avner Cohen and Marvin Miller recommend that Israel "cap its production of weapons-usable nuclear materials, while the Arab states and Iran should reinforce their declaratory commitment not to produce nuclear weapons by accepting the authority of the IAEA to make special inspections at both declared and suspect nuclear facilities." They also claim that this formula has been endorsed "informally by a senior Israeli nuclear analyst." "How to Think About—and Implement—Nuclear Arms Control in the Middle East," *The Washington Quarterly,* Spring, 1993, p. 110. From the Israeli perspective, this is a non-starter, and no government official has endorsed this proposal. Any "bargain" based on the combination of declaratory commitments from Iran and Libya and the authority of the IAEA, are, as explained in this paper, unacceptable.

Implementation and Verification

8 Modalities for Verifying a Middle East Nuclear-Weapon-Free Zone

Lawrence Scheinman

INTRODUCTION

Political realities, even with the Madrid peace process and an increasing sense that responsible political leaders in the region see and would like to capitalize on the opportunity to break the long impasse in Middle East regional relations, strongly suggest that a Middle East Nuclear-Weapon-Free Zone (MENWFZ) is still a good distance away. Even the sudden signing of peace treaties recognizing Israel's legitimacy, establishing undisputed borders, and opening diplomatic relations, would not suffice to radically change the prognosis for a long wait for a nuclear-weapon-free Middle East. The scars of the past are etched deeply in the consciousness of states and peoples in the region. It will take time and a positive record of cooperation, peace, and perhaps even the consolidation of liberal democratic political systems to bring about the preferred outcome.

But time is a precious commodity, and it is clear that if it is the interest of the states of the region to foreclose regional nuclearization and ensure that nuclear weapons are excluded, the process has to begin now. A NWFZ could come in stages; could be built incrementally beginning with confidence-building measures that are nuclear-specific. While one or more of these could be unilateral acts, they would be stronger if incorporated in a formalized instrument. A number come to mind:

first, capping production of weapons-usable material;

second, agreeing not to import or domestically develop facilities capable of producing weapons-usable materials;

third, agreeing that if such facilities should, in the future, appear to be relevant for peaceful nuclear development, they would have to be multinationally owned and operated (either regionally or with participation of outside states) under stringent international controls and safeguards and linked to international fissile material storage and management arrangements.

It would seem certain that the security of supply of resources, technology and equipment relevant to operating peaceful nuclear activities would have to be assured if the parties to such exclusion provisions were to find them acceptable, and therefore this confidence-building measure might reasonably be linked to appropriate supply assurances.

Fourth, regional states already under full-scope safeguards could explore the possibility of a program of *invitational* inspections whereby each state with a nuclear program under safeguards invites verification authorities—in this case the IAEA since comprehensive safeguards are already a function of NPT membership—to make one or more annual visits *above* and *beyond* routine inspections to any location the IAEA may choose, due allowance being made for protecting commercial and non-nuclear activities relevant to national security of the inviting state.[1] The number of invited visits could be keyed to criteria concerning the size and character of the safeguarded nuclear programs.

Fifth, facilities that are shut down, whether or not in a full-scope safeguarded state, could be placed under IAEA safeguards that are implemented in a way to minimize intrusion but to ensure compliance. This would serve the interest of establishing and maintaining some degree of equalization of responsibility and burden among the regional states involved, irrespective of their NPT or full-scope safeguards status. The fourth and fifth measures are reciprocal but not necessarily in the sense of conditionality: the fourth involves NPT parties while the fifth clearly focuses on the Dimona reactor in Israel. The measures could be taken unilaterally and without explicitly requiring a reciprocal measure, or they could be taken in consequence of a mutual agreement of reciprocity.

A *sixth* measure could entail agreement not to conduct any nuclear explosions for any purpose whatsoever, including so-called peaceful nuclear explosions. With a comprehensive test ban now under active negotiation, this would seem to be a relatively easy agreement to achieve.

These are beginning steps only—but they are important ones. They are measures that could be considered now and implemented in the near term. As in the case of progress toward peace in the Middle East generally, there is now a window of opportunity. Failure now may mean a very bleak and dangerous future for the region and for the international community. Steps that can avert that kind of an outcome can and should be taken. Not to try would be irresponsible.

SOME BASIC PROPOSITIONS

Nuclear-weapon-free zones (NWFZ) are arms control agreements designed to ensure the total absence of nuclear weapons from the territories of the states covered by the agreement. In this respect they go further than the Treaty on the Nonproliferation of Nuclear Weapons (NPT), which seeks to prohibit the spread of nuclear weapons beyond the five acknowledged nuclear weapon states but does not foreclose the deployment by nuclear weapon states of weapons under their control on the territories of non-nuclear weapon state àllies. NWFZ, on the other hand, prohibit the presence, subject to rights of innocent passage, archipelagic sea lane passage, and transit passage of straits, of *any* nuclear weapons, regardless of who exercises authority or control over them in the state or on territory under its control.

Nuclear-weapon-free zones have been established in both uninhabited (Antarctic, Outer Space, Seabed) and inhabited (Latin America, South Pacific) areas. The latter two are of particular relevance to the examination of a verification regime for an eventual Middle East NWFZ. Both the Latin American NWFZ (established by the Treaty of Tlatelolco in 1967) and the South Pacific NWFZ (established by the Treaty of Rarotonga in 1986) cover large populated areas and are designed to prevent the further spread of nuclear weapons. Although largely similar, there are some differences between them. Whereas Tlatelolco makes allowance for the possibility of peaceful nuclear explosions, Rarotonga, like the NPT, does not. Rarotonga applies up to the twelve mile territorial sea limit whereas Tlatelolco forecloses the deployment of nuclear weapons on oceans adjacent to the territorial sea. Rarotonga regulates dumping of nuclear waste at sea; Tlatelolco does not. Both treaties contain protocols providing for the nuclear weapon states to respect the denuclearization of the zone and to commit themselves to negative security assurances (i.e., commitments not to use or threaten to use nuclear weapons against any non-nuclear weapon state party). Both treaties provide for IAEA verification of the non-diversion of nuclear material, and both provide for the establishment of regional institutions (OPANAL in the case of Tlatelolco; the Consultative Committee in the case of Rarotonga[2]) to deal with compliance problems.

The creation of other zones has been under discussion for some time. There has been significant progress toward concluding a NWFZ in Africa south of the Sahara since South Africa joined the NPT and submitted to full-scope IAEA safeguards. A Southeast Asian NWFZ is also being actively pursued. The establishment of a NWFZ in the Middle East, or even more broadly a zone free of all weapons of mass destruction including missile delivery systems, has been on the agenda for some years. Most states in the region, including Israel, agree on its desirability in principle, while differing on the modalities and conditions for realizing it.

Achievement of a Middle East NWFZ has taken on added urgency in the wake of revelations regarding the Iraqi nuclear weapon development program. The relevant U.N. Security Council Resolution (687) set out a number of goals for Iraq, several of which are also regarded as steps toward the broader goal of establishing a Middle East zone free of weapons of mass destruction. Among these are:

a.   no acquisition or development of nuclear weapons,
b.   no production of weapons-usable nuclear material, and
c.   no development of subsystems or components related to weapons or weapons-usable material.

While the first is identical with NPT, Tlatelolco and Rarotonga goals, the second and third are more far-reaching. The United States Middle East proposals (May, 1991), which remain valid today, also included a call for a NWFZ and for the cessation of production anywhere in the region of weapons-usable nuclear material.

A consideration of alternative arrangements for verifying an eventual NWFZ in the Middle East should begin with three basic propositions.

First, to provide the necessary degree of credibility, a verification regime must be correlated with the obligations, compliance with which are central to the success of the basic agreement.

Second, nuclear-weapon-free zones, while regional in character, are part of the global nonproliferation regime. The provision in Article VII of the NPT accommodating regional zones explicitly recognizes this relationship.

Third, participants in a regional agreement may have a specific set of concerns that need to be addressed and may as a result set forth particular obligations not necessarily found in the global non-proliferation regime. These in turn may require special verification arrangements which are more complex or intrusive than those applied at the global level. Even so, these arrangements must be understood as *complementary and additive* and not as substitutes for international verification. International verification must be accepted as the *sine qua non* for nuclear non-proliferation. Overall verification arrangements for the zone must not just satisfy the zonal participants but also the broader international community. Against this background, we may consider the possible obligations that might be included in a Middle East NWFZ agreement, the degree of verification that might be required to provide confidence that undertakings are being fulfilled by the parties, and institutional arrangements that might be established to implement verification requirements.

OBLIGATIONS

The obligations of three groups of states must be considered in the case of a Middle East NWFZ: first, states that are located in the zone and that would be parties to a NWFZ treaty; second, nuclear weapon states and other extra-regional states with jurisdictional responsibilities within the boundaries of the defined zone; and third, supplier states from which exports—ranging from material through components and parts to full-scale facilities—might be obtained. With respect to the zonal participants, three categories of obligation can be identified:

a.   those excluding possession, acquisition or manufacture of nuclear weapons or nuclear explosive devices;

b. those foreclosing research and development related to nuclear weapons or explosives; and

c. those requiring disclosure of all nuclear activities and the application of international safeguards.

Subject to more detailed discussion in the following section, the obligations for states located in the zone can be identified as follows:

under a:

1. renunciation of the possession, or acquisition of, or control over nuclear weapons and nuclear explosive devices;

2. renunciation of the use of nuclear explosives of any kind for any purpose whatsoever;

3. commitment not to receive or to seek any assistance in the manufacture or acquisition of nuclear weapons or nuclear explosive devices;

4. commitment not to carry out any nuclear weapons related research and development;

5. commitment not to permit the deployment or testing of nuclear weapons or nuclear explosive devices anywhere in their territory;

6. commitment to use nuclear energy for exclusively peaceful, non-explosive purposes;

under b:

7. undertaking not to produce (i.e., enrich or reprocess) any nuclear materials that are usable in nuclear weapons or nuclear explosive devices;

8. commitment not to engage in any research and development related to nuclear weapon material on their territory or anywhere else under their control;

9. commitment not to stockpile any weapons-usable material, wherever produced, on their territory;

under c:

10. undertake to account for and to place under international auspices and control any existing stocks of weapons-usable nuclear material;

11. commitment to accept safeguards on all nuclear material and installations located on their territory or under their control;

12. report all imports, exports and production of nuclear material, equipment, plant and technology;

13. provide an annual report on all nuclear-related research and development;

14. insofar as IAEA safeguards are involved (which will continue regardless of what new or additional verification arrangements are established in the context of a nuclear-weapon-free zone):

    [a] acceptance by all states in the zone of all inspectors designated by the IAEA or safeguards responsibilities as well as commitments to take prompt action on proposed designations by the IAEA and to avoid restrictive policies on the numbers and nationalities of designated inspectors;

    [b] acceptance by all states in the zone of the principle of multiple entry, long-duration visas so that inspections can be conducted without delay, and any short-notice or unannounced inspections can be conducted in a manner designed to engender confidence in the system;

[c] provision for resident inspection at agreed-upon sites in zonal states;

[d] acceptance of IAEA right to perform unannounced inspections and inspections at short notice.

A NWFZ agreement could be established all at once or in stages. In the latter event, which is more probable for the Middle East, the agreement could initially extend to one or more, or even all, present and future nuclear activity. An example would be the capping of production of fissile material and the shutting down of production facilities that now exist. This could be verified by using seals at selected points and periodically verifying the integrity of the seal—an activity that could be very *unobtrusive*. Past activity, including the production of nuclear material, could be kept separate in the first instance and brought under coverage according to the improvement of political relations or according to a timetable mutually agreed by the regional parties.

It also matters that states outside the region—both nuclear weapon states and non-weapon supplier states—cooperate with and support regional efforts. For nuclear weapon states obligations might include:

a.   respecting the nuclear weapon free status of the zone and of the parties to the zonal arrangement in all respects agreed to by the zonal parties;

b.   not contributing in any way to any violation of the treaty;

c.   providing assurances to all parties to the treaty that they will not use or threaten to use nuclear weapons against any of them (negative security assurances);

d.   providing assurances that if any NWFZ party is attacked or under threat of attack by another state having nuclear

weapons, they will come to the assistance of the
threatened state or states (positive security assurances);

e. providing the IAEA (and any regional control body) any
    information that might be indicative or suggestive of a
    safeguards or reporting violation. (Any state, not just
    nuclear-weapon states, could make such an undertaking).

Finally, extra-regional non-nuclear-weapon state obligations
could include not taking actions that would undermine or defeat
the objectives related to renunciation of nuclear weapons or
nuclear explosive devices and to excluding the presence or
production of weapons-usable materials, even for peaceful
purposes, on the territories of the states in the region as well as
not doing anything to encourage or facilitate research and
development in restricted areas of activity. Extra-regional non-
nuclear states could undertake not to export any items or
components that zonal parties agreed not to import (e.g., items
related to reprocessing or enrichment if an agreement were to be
reached to exclude these capabilities from the region) and to
report all exports and nuclear related transactions with states
party to the zonal agreement. Exporting states could go even
further and require safeguards on all exports of all plant and
equipment, and report all transfers of dual-use equipment or
machinery to NWFZ participants.

VERIFICATION REQUIREMENTS

Effective verification is essential to confidence-building and
arms control. The term "effective" is not easily defined. At a
minimum it has a military and a political component. Political
criteria may be more difficult to satisfy than military criteria:
failure to meet political criteria may result in a loss of
confidence which can have far-reaching impact, whereas failure
to satisfy military criteria may be irrelevant if the political
authorities are satisfied with the level of verified compliance. In

the case of the Middle East, where insecurity is high, stability low, and distrust widespread, political criteria would be especially important. It would therefore seem inevitable that in the Middle East verification arrangements more far-reaching than any of the safeguards approaches heretofore applied by the IAEA will be required and that a combination of verification strategies will need to be devised.

Several states in the region have, in fact, already underlined the need for mutual and binding reassurances between participating states, meaning that some form of mutual inspection above and beyond any international verification that might be involved would be a necessary element of an acceptable regime, at least in the formative years of a nuclear-weapon-free zone. This suggests a very substantial emphasis on regional verification approaches.

However, nuclear-weapon-free zones are of relevance not only to the parties directly involved but also to states bordering the region and the wider international community. This is particularly the case in the Middle East, which is generally regarded not only as one of the most volatile regions of the world, but one where the outbreak of violence could have far-reaching international implications. This underscores the need for credible international verification of a NWFZ in which there could be general confidence, in addition to any regional verification arrangements that might be agreed by the parties directly involved in a regional treaty.

As discussed earlier, the obligations which might be part of a nuclear-weapon-free zone treaty resolve into three general categories:

    a.   those which exclude the possession, acquisition, or manufacture of nuclear weapons or nuclear explosive devices;

b. those which foreclose research and development, production, importing or stockpiling of directly weapons-usable materials; and

c. those which require the application of safeguards to all nuclear material, installations and activities in the region, as well as full disclosure of all nuclear activities, including imports, exports, production, and basic research and development.

The obligations on excluding possession, acquisition, or manufacture of nuclear weapons or explosive devices already have been incurred by the many states in the Middle East that have joined the NPT. All of those states which have significant nuclear activity have concluded the required comprehensive safeguards agreements with the IAEA. The remainder are under obligation to conclude safeguards agreements with the Agency. Even without becoming a party to the NPT, states can conclude comprehensive safeguards agreements with the IAEA as Albania did prior to becoming a member of the NPT and as Argentina and Brazil have done through the quadripartite agreement between themselves, the Argentine–Brazilian Agency for Accounting and Control of Nuclear Material (ABACC) and the IAEA.

These NPT-type safeguards cover all nuclear material in peaceful nuclear activity in those states. In addition, states are required to notify the IAEA of any nuclear facility under construction and of any modification of any existing facility at least 180 days before nuclear material is introduced.[3] However, assurance that no research and development related to nuclear explosives is taking place, or that a state has not acquired a nuclear explosive device from outside, or that no covert weapons-related activity whatsoever—even if material is not yet involved—was being conducted on the territory of a state party to a nuclear-weapon-free zone agreement would require verification activities beyond that which has traditionally been applied by the IAEA. The requisite assurance that no nuclear weapon related activity of any sort was taking place could require invoking mutual reassurance measures by the parties directly involved and directly concerned. While international verification authorities could play a significant role in bringing about that assurance, political considerations may require additional verification activities carried out by regional or national authorities.

It is important to consider that whether international, regional, or bilateral, there are limits to just how effective verification can be. The introduction of a regional verification authority should not be seen as a panacea. It is also worth considering that international systems may be able to draw upon a wider array of resources (data bases, information exchanges, national technical means information made available by states invested with those capabilities, open skies arrangements) than regional arrangements, which may be constrained by more limited resources. The effectiveness of verification may in the long run be measured in terms of the integration of a cross-section of verification methods and procedures rather than just in the ability of a country to gain access by challenge inspections to sites in a neighboring state.

The obligations foreclosing research and development, production, importation, or stockpiling of directly weapons-usable materials go beyond what is currently required in any international or regional nonproliferation arrangement, although they are to be found among the measures required to be applied in Iraq under Security Council Resolution 687 and also provided for in the December, 1991 bilateral agreement between North and South Korea. Pursuant to its mandate under U.N. SCR687 to establish a plan for ongoing monitoring and verification of Iraq's compliance with that resolution, the IAEA has established a monitoring plan based on the assumption that all nuclear material, equipment, installations, and relevant non-nuclear material will be subject to ongoing verification, including arrangements for full and free access at any time to all locations and information necessary to effectively conduct monitoring activity. Such arrangements could be extended throughout the region in the unlikely event that the parties to a NWFZ so decided, but the emphasis given to mutual reassurance may lead to demands for far-reaching arrangements for access and inspection that go beyond even the enhanced verification involved in Security Council Resolution 687. And parties to such an agreement may conclude that for it to be effectively implemented, newly defined undertakings not presently covered by existing verification arrangements require new institutions and procedures.

Insofar as the obligations requiring application of safeguards to all nuclear materials, installations and activities as well as full disclosure of all nuclear activities including imports, exports, production, and basic research are concerned, states under comprehensive safeguards agreements already are required to submit all material in peaceful nuclear activity to IAEA verification. As for installations which do not contain nuclear material, although NPT-type safeguards are not applied at such facilities, the right to verify installations, equipment and non-nuclear material could be given to the Agency with each state obligated to provide a comprehensive inventory of all such facilities, equipment, or non-nuclear material. As well, responsibility for implementing verification of compliance with obligations related to these elements could be assigned to a regional monitoring institution. Once again, the scope and reach of verification activity would be enlarged beyond current practice as more obligations were assumed by parties to agreements restricting the nature of legitimate activity in a given region.

INSTITUTIONAL ALTERNATIVES

Against the background of these considerations, several verification options can be identified for a Middle East NWFZ. Given what has been said about the emphasis on mutual and binding assurances as a basic condition for achieving progress toward a NWFZ in the Middle East, some combination of international and regional approaches is indicated. Four alternatives for allocating verification responsibility between international and regional authority can be identified:

A. Verification Responsibility Option: Place all *routine* verification responsibility in the hands of the IAEA, consistent with the arrangements and procedures applied pursuant to comprehensive safeguards agreements.

This could be accompanied by an arrangement for designated regional personnel to participate as observers in the conducting of on-site inspections. *Non-routine* verification—i.e., verification activities triggered by:

1. special requests either of the party to be investigated, or

2. a party to the regional agreement pursuant to treaty provisions, or

3. the verifying authority itself, due to inability to reach conclusions regarding material, plant or equipment subject to safeguards verification, or

4. even a non-zonal state such as a nuclear weapon state or a supplier state, could be conducted either by:

   [a] the IAEA alone,

   [b] the IAEA with regionally-designated observers,

   [c] a joint team consisting of IAEA and regional inspectors, or

[d] a regional inspection team designated by the appropriate regional authority and authorized to conduct inspections triggered by special circumstances.

This model builds on existing international verification arrangements as carried out by the IAEA while accommodating regional verification authorities as passive participants with respect to routine verification activities but as active participants with respect to any non-routine activities. Special inspections, including so-called "challenge inspections" such as are provided for in both the Tlatelolco and Raratonga treaties, could be conducted jointly by international and regional authorities, either dividing inspection responsibilities between them and then pooling and sharing all information gathered as well as the results of subsequent analysis or carrying out parallel but independent full inspections and sharing the results of later analysis. (Pursuant to amendments to the Treaty of Tlatelolco proposed by Argentina and Brazil August, 1992, special inspections are now the responsibility of the IAEA rather than the Agency for the Prohibition of Nuclear Weapons in Latin America [OPANAL].) The regional team could consist of members of a formal regional inspectorate operating in some agreed-upon relationship with the IAEA, or if no formal inspectorate existed, of persons selected by an appropriate regional authority from among member states of the zone.

B. Verification Responsibility Option: All *routine* verification to be conducted *jointly* by international and regional verification authorities. *Non-routine* verification (as defined above) to be carried out either on the same basis as routine verification or by the regional authority alone.

This alternative involves a formal, structured, two-tier verification arrangement. Two examples currently exist of such an arrangement, the European Atomic Energy Community (EURATOM) and the Argentine–Brazilian Agency for Accounting and Control of Nuclear Material (ABACC), although in neither case does the regional authority exercise sole authority with respect to non-routine verification activities.[4] In both cases safeguards agreements with the IAEA include Protocols which specify in a detailed manner the scope and character of cooperation between the regional and international verification authorities. This approach involves the establishing of a formal regional authority and the creation of a regional inspectorate.

Many of the observations made in discussing the previous alternative apply here as well. However under this approach the rights and obligations of the regional and international authority would be spelled out in full. Insofar as routine inspection is concerned, the main question would be whether both inspectorates would perform essentially the same functions (which as the EURATOM experience demonstrates entails duplication and added cost) or whether the verification regime would be made more labor-efficient and cost-effective through some distribution of responsibilities. Whatever choice was made, it would be important that each verification authority would be able to reach independent conclusions regarding compliance and that neither the effectiveness nor the credibility of either system be compromised in any way.

ABACC may be a better touchstone for this alternative than EURATOM, involving as it does countries which are emerging from a period of political tension (although not military hostility), which remain political rivals, and which are not parties to the NPT. While not identical to the Middle East and in some ways quite different (e.g., the concern in the case of Argentina and Brazil might be collusion, whereas the concern in the Middle East is confrontation), ABACC's background has more similarities with the situation in the Middle East than does EURATOM's.

ABACC administers and implements a Common System of Accounting and Control of Nuclear Materials (SCCC), established by Argentina and Brazil pursuant to their November, 1990 Declaration of Common Nuclear Policy. The following observations on ABACC are relevant:

1. Unlike the NPT, there is no provision in ABACC (or the Tlatelolco Treaty for that matter) allowing for non-proscribed military use of nuclear material, although both make allowance for nuclear propulsion and for arranging special procedures for the temporary non-application of safeguards when material is in such use.

2. The ABACC–IAEA Protocol, which is modeled on the IAEA–EURATOM agreement but which is a second generation document that reflects experience acquired in implementing the EURATOM agreement, emphasizes the need for both institutions to reach their own independent conclusions, to coordinate activities "to the extent possible," to work jointly "where feasible," and to "enable the Agency to fulfill its obligations." (Article 1)

For routine purposes (collecting information and reports) ABACC functions *vis-à-vis* the IAEA as a state system of accounting for and control of nuclear material. Routine IAEA inspections take account of ABACC inspection activities but are mindful of the need for the Agency to be able to fulfill its obligations and reach independent conclusions.

3. No special provisions are made for special inspections; the agreement includes the standard provisions of INFCIRC/153[5] in this regard.

As noted earlier, amendment of Tlatelolco has the effect of shifting special inspection responsibility from OPANAL to the IAEA. Nevertheless, it is possible for an arrangement to be agreed which, while preserving IAEA special inspection rights also establishes procedures for regional authorities to either accompany IAEA on such inspections, and share information, findings and analysis, or to conduct additional special or challenge inspections in the state.

under either Option A or B above, the parties to a nuclear-weapon-free zone could consider incorporating a system of *quota* inspections *in addition* to (*not* as a substitute for) routine and special inspections. They could agree that a certain number of inspections could be carried out on demand each year at any location in a state or at designated locations. Demand could be made by any member state or by the regional organization that anchors the zonal agreement. It would be agreed beforehand that any inspector on a designated list of inspectors (which the states would previously have approved) could be sent, and that access would be provided immediately upon request and that the inspectors would be transported without delay to any designated site. This kind of inspection arrangement could be made the responsibility of an international inspectorate, but it is more likely that the states involved would prefer regional inspectors for such tasks. However, an IAEA inspector could be invited to participate as an observer to the quota inspections in the interest of ensuring maximum continuity of information and knowledge and of optimizing the principle of transparency which is important to confidence-building. An arrangement of this type was basic to the INF agreement concluded in 1988 between the United States and the Soviet Union.

   C. Verification Responsibility Option: Regions grant the right and obligation to verify independently, with all *routine* verification activity conducted by inspectors designated by a regional authority but with the international verification authority retaining the right to participate as an observer. *Non-routine* verification activity would be conducted by the regional authority alone (or possibly again with observer participation by the international verification authority).

This alternative places principal responsibility in the hands of regional authorities. It is assumed that in this circumstance, a regional inspectorate would have been created by the regional authority to implement and administer verification activities and that both routine and non-routine situations would fall in the domain of the regional authority. As noted, under this arrangement it would still be possible to include international inspectors in some or all of the regional inspectorate's activities but as passive observers, not as active participants. under this scenario the international authority would not be able to conduct separate activities in the interest of independent verification but at most would be verifying the effectiveness of the regional inspectorate.

This option is not discussed in detail since, as elaborated in the introduction to this chapter, any arrangement that limited effective verification to the regional authorities alone probably would not be adequate to meet the concerns of the broader international community; namely, that nuclear weapons proliferation—or creation of the capability to rapidly gain nuclear weapons—was not being carried out in the states covered by the nuclear-weapon-free zone arrangement.

Failure to involve the IAEA, as a representative of the international community, in effective verification of a regional nuclear-weapon-free-zone arrangement would be potentially damaging not only to the safeguards system of the IAEA (part of whose credibility depends on the extent to which it is universally applied) but also to the nonproliferation regime of which the international verification system is a fundamental part. Regional arrangements that serve as confidence-building measures are undoubtedly critical to acceptable arrangements in some parts of the world and may be the condition *sine qua non* for achieving effective nonproliferation, but this cannot be at the expense of international verification and internationally binding arrangements among the relevant parties.

D. Verification Responsibility Option: Independent (and simultaneous) verification could be carried out by a mutual inspection body created by and responsible to a political authority consisting of the immediate parties to the regional agreement, and by the IAEA on behalf of the international community (and the parties to the zonal agreement).

An arrangement of this type is envisioned in the Joint Declaration for a Non-Nuclear Korean Peninsula (agreed 31 December, 1991). This alternative involves a bilateral system of mutual reassurance rather than a multilateral system. Each of two parties acquires rights and obligations *vis-à-vis* the other to verify to its satisfaction that all undertakings relative to the non-development of nuclear weapons, and in the case of the Korean peninsula nuclear weapons material as well, are being observed. What is involved here is clearly an intensive system of mutual verification. Attributes of this kind of mutual inspection are highly relevant to the Middle East where mutuality of rights and obligations are a major concern.

The observations made regarding Option C apply here as well: however comprehensive and far-reaching the regional verification arrangements may be, they cannot be considered as functional equivalents to or substitutes for international verification. That level of verification remains essential in the interest of the nonproliferation regime and the international community at large.

In both Option C and Option D, therefore, the role of the international verification authority cannot be significantly different from the role that it plays in regard to any full-scope safeguards arrangement. However, particular responsibilities, as in the case of Option II, can be vested in regional authorities alone or in conjunction with the IAEA.

Whichever approach is used, to the extent that the IAEA is involved, the comprehensive safeguards document INFCIRC/ 153 would serve as the basis for IAEA involvement. While certain matters discussed in that circular including, the basic undertaking (para. 1), cooperation between the agency and the state or multilateral entity (para. 3), the system of accounting and control (para. 7), and agency inspectors (para. 9) would be tailored to meet the particular requirements of the nuclear-weapon-free zone agreement, the main provisions of INFCIRC/153 Part II, together with matters related to privileges and immunities, sharing of costs, liability, and settlement of disputes, would generally apply.

CONCLUSION

This discussion of verification alternatives serves to confirm that where there is political will to agree to formal constraints on state behavior, tools are available to verify compliance with undertakings. Verification can be carried out bilaterally, regionally, or internationally by combining different levels of verification to meet particular requirements of the parties to a non-proliferation agreement. We have argued here that while international verification arrangements may not be suited to meet all of the requirements of regional parties, regional arrangements may be insufficient to provide the confidence and credibility that states outside the region may require if they are to be satisfied that their security interests are being served and supported by the regional nonproliferation agreement. In cases such as the Middle East, hybrid approaches involving several levels of verification may make the most sense.

However, the main point is that adequate, reliable verification regimes that command credibility, build confidence, and serve the interest of security and stability can be devised and implemented if the fundamental ingredient of political will to achieve nonproliferation is in place. Verification does not create that political will; it only helps to reinforce it and to enable the engaged parties to move forward on the road to stability and peace.

NOTES

1. A Chemical Weapons Convention provision for managed access in certain cases involving challenge-type inspections—a more far-reaching concept than that being proposed here—could be relevant to inspections by invitation.

2. OPANAL, the Agency for the Prohibition of Nuclear Weapons in Latin America, is the institution provided for in the Treaty of Tlatelolco to ensure compliance with the Treaty. Its special inspection responsibility has been transferred to the IAEA pursuant to an amendment to the Treaty co-sponsored by Argentina and Brazil. The Consultative Committee of the Treaty of Rarotonga consists of all parties to the treaty and is intended to deal with any issues arising out of the treaty regarding operation, interpretation, or amendment.

3. In 1992 the IAEA Board of Governers decided that the requirement that design information be transmitted to the Agency "as early as possible" meant at the time of decision and not 180 days before actual introduction of material into the facility. This gives the Agency considerable early notice of nuclear activity not involving nuclear material and is an important step in ensuring increased transparency on national nuclear activity.

4. EURATOM is the European Atomic Energy Community, created in 1957 along with the European Economic Community (EEC), both of which are now known as the European Union (EU). EURATOM received special consideration from the United States and others in terms of verification responsibilities in view of its multinational character and relationship to achieving European political inategration. Consequently, its arrangements with the IAEA differ somewhat from those of individual states contracting safeguards agreements with the IAEA. But in all cases, safeguards agreements

must ensure that the IAEA can independently verify that all nuclear material under safeguards can be accounted for. ABACC, the Argentine–Brazilian Agency for Accounting and Control of Nuclear Material, is modelled after EURATOM but takes into account lessons learned from the IAEA–EURATOM experience of more than 15 years and makes adjustments accordingly.

5. INFCIRC/153 is the basic IAEA safeguards document upon which all full-scope safeguards agreements, whether deriving from the NPT, regional nuclear-weapon-free zone treaties or from unilateral submission to full-scope safeguards, are based.

9   The Role of Technology in Regional Security

Arian Pregenzer and John Taylor

INTRODUCTION

In this chapter we propose that technology can play an important role in facilitating regional security in the Middle East. The proposal is based on the understanding that solutions to regional security problems are political in nature, not technical, and that technology can provide no magical solution. However, technology has successfully facilitated political agreements in bilateral, multilateral, and regional contexts in the past. Examples include the withdrawal of troops from the Sinai in the 1970s; agreement between the United States and the Soviet Union on the treaty banning Intermediate Range Nuclear Forces (INF) in 1989; and the multilateral Chemical Weapons Convention (CWC) which opened for signature in 1993.

Importance of Communication

An understanding of both the capabilities and limitations of monitoring technology could assist negotiators with decision making throughout the negotiating process. For example, during consideration of an agreement to ban missile test flights, negotiators would need to understand the extent to which the terms of the agreement could be verified. If negotiators knew that compliance with a ban on missile flights could be monitored, they might be more willing to consider such an agreement; conversely, an inability to monitor compliance with agreements might lead to changes in the negotiated agreement. After an agreement is reached, knowledge about verification technologies is also essential: working out the details of verification or monitoring regimes and their subsequent implementation often requires significant input from technical experts.

Communication works both ways, however. Just as knowledge about the capabilities of verification technologies may facilitate the political process, knowledge about the issues involved in a particular negotiation helps steer technology along relevant paths. The ability of technology to have successful impact on a particular agreement is enhanced by communication between the political and technical communities early in the negotiating process. The significant lead-times associated with implementing or developing technological solutions is another reason why early involvement by the technical community can be beneficial.

Types of Technology

In the context of this chapter, the term "technology" will be used in a broad sense and will include instrumentation, equipment, algorithms, and software as well as technical analysis and technical processes. Examples include unattended ground sensor systems, aerial overflight systems, satellite systems, image processing interfaces, information management and data fusion systems, data security systems, portable inspector equipment, and methods for on-site inspection. Use of these technologies facilitates implementation of agreements by providing the capability to observe activities of concern, to define and measure agreed parameters, to record and manage information, and to carry out agreed-upon inspections.

In addition to the obvious technical advantages gained by the appropriate use of technology, its use also serves to depersonalize the process of compliance monitoring by providing timely access to objective data. Availability to all parties to an agreement of standardized monitoring systems balances their ability to detect significant activities and thereby contributes to an atmosphere of mutual trust and peaceful resolution of conflict.

Organization of the Chapter

This chapter proposes a program for evaluating appropriate applications of technology to facilitate the Middle East peace process. The program consists of four parts: an issues analysis and specification of technical requirements; the need for technical exchange and demonstrations of relevant technologies; the uses of modeling and simulation; and development of a Cooperative Monitoring Center. Following these discussions, we examine the use of technology in two hypothetical monitoring scenarios: monitoring an agreement to restrict tank movement near a garrison and monitoring troop movement through a chokepoint or across a boundary. A summary and conclusions follow these discussions.

ISSUES ANALYSIS AND SPECIFICATION OF TECHNICAL REQUIREMENTS

A necessary part of any program that introduces verification and monitoring technology into the Middle East peace process is understanding possible regional applications, potential users of the technology, technical requirements, and the development of a reasonable set of hypothetical monitoring scenarios. Such analysis requires joint involvement of the technical and political communities, including representatives from the affected regions.

Applications and Users

Possible applications of technology include verifying regional or bilateral treaties or agreements, monitoring the progress of confidence-building measures (CBMs), or monitoring the status of military deployments. The degree of permitted intrusiveness will influence the choice of technology system. In addition, the needs and characteristics of the eventual user of the technology must be considered. Export controls must be figured into any proposal to transfer technology to regional users, whereas in some cases, monitoring by a third party might avoid problems with exportability. Sometimes the user has definite requirements for simplicity and ease of use that cannot be ignored; for example, the type of vehicles available to transport monitoring teams may preclude use of technology that is not easily portable. Similarly, if the user is an established multilateral or regional organization, permanent regional monitoring facilities or communication centers could be acceptable, whereas an individual user from a specific country might require far more portability. Some decisions about the regional application and the eventual user must guide the process of proposing technologies.

Monitoring Scenarios

Development of a hypothetical set of monitoring scenarios is another necessary component to any proposal concerning technologies. Given a particular application and user, a concrete example of an agreement or confidence-building measure must be assumed before appropriate technologies can be proposed. Whereas most technologies might have some applicability to many scenarios, efficiency and minimum intrusiveness require that each scenario be considered separately. For example, although chemical sampling, satellite imagery, and unattended ground sensors might be relevant to monitoring the closure of a production facility, very high confidence in the facility's closure might be obtained solely from the judicious use of tamper indicating seals at critical points in the production process, provided that inspectors can make periodic visits to check the seals. If inspections were deemed too intrusive, other options would warrant consideration. Again, involvement by knowledgeable participants from the region will be critical to the credibility of both the scenario and any proposed technology system.

Identifying Monitoring Technologies

Once a set of monitoring scenarios has been developed, appropriate systems of technologies can be identified. This would include both verification technologies such as sensors, tags, seals, and communication systems as well as information and data processing systems. The use of modeling and simulation technologies could aid in optimizing sensor selection, deployment and synergy. To facilitate the transfer of information among parties and from extra-regional participants to the parties, techniques to enable the sharing of intelligence and sensitive information will need to be developed.

Synergism with Other Monitoring Applications

Finally, consideration of the applicability of verification and monitoring technologies to other areas of concern would enhance the impact and efficiency of the system. For example, multi-spectral thermal imagery from satellite monitoring might be relevant to environmental studies on desertification or water resource management. This would require coordination with other working groups in the multilateral peace process.

TECHNICAL EXCHANGE AND DEMONSTRATIONS

As stressed in the introduction, communication between the political and technical communities increases the effectiveness of both. Demonstrations of unclassified, exportable monitoring technologies would both increase awareness of the capabilities (and limitations) of verification monitoring technologies and facilitate the analysis of regional issues and technical requirements. Such demonstrations could occur either in individual countries in the region or at a neutral location outside the region, such as the United States.

Another way of establishing communication between the technical and political groups would be to assign technical advisors to the multilateral and bilateral talks. These technical advisors would serve the dual purpose of advising negotiators and funneling relevant information to technologists responsible for developing monitoring systems.

To foster cooperation among the technical communities in the United States and the Middle East, joint research programs could be pursued, accompanied by collaborations between universities, laboratories, and other institutions.

MODELING AND SIMULATION

The term "modeling and simulation" refers to a variety of activities, including use of computer models to simulate sensor response to physical phenomena, the use of transportation models to simulate troop movements and their interaction with sensors, system-level physical or computer modeling of optimal sensor deployment and synergy, and facility modeling for purposes of planning on-site inspections or monitoring. In this sense, modeling and simulation can be thought of as a low-risk, and relatively low-cost, developmental tool. For example, if the parties to a treaty are considering using ground-based sensors to track heavy vehicular traffic in a mountainous terrain, some computer or physical modeling of the situation can allow experimentation and optimization with various combinations and configurations of sensors prior to actual deployment. For some situations, simple physical modeling may be sufficient; however, for complex combinations of sensors and large spatial dimensions, computer modeling may be desirable. Computer modeling would be of particular value for optimizing the synergistic effect of a variety of sensors or for testing the response of particular sensors to simulated physical phenomena.

In addition to these more traditional applications, modeling and simulation might provide a way of understanding the effects of proposed confidence-building measures or agreements prior to their approval. For example, traditional war games might be altered to allow for the simulated implementation of troop or equipment withdrawals from particular regions, including methods to monitor the withdrawal. Such a "peace game" might be useful in determining how such measures would affect national security of the concerned parties. It could perhaps test the fairness or impartiality of such measures and suggest flaws or enhancements prior to actually entering into the agreement.

The capability to model physical processes already exists to a large degree within many monitoring technology programs. However, the ability to model sensor deployment in a variety of physical situations needs significant development. Similarly, the capability of modeling the effects of confidence-building measures, or "peace gaming," lies in the future. Interaction between the technical and political communities could be useful in steering future developments.

COOPERATIVE MONITORING CENTER

In addition to demonstrations, simulations, and technology exchanges, a center outside the region and designed to allow participants to experiment with different combinations of monitoring systems could facilitate the process of achieving regional security in the Middle East. Such a center, here referred to as a Cooperative Monitoring Center (CMC), would allow participants to get hands-on experience with monitoring hardware and data, computer simulations and modeling, information management and data fusion techniques, and joint or third party monitoring processes. The center would provide access to a wide variety of monitoring systems, such as airborne, satellite, and ground-based systems, as well as a communications center which would receive sensor data and other input and would incorporate data fusion, display, and archiving capabilities. The center would also include modeling and simulation capabilities both to assist in designing monitoring systems and as a possible tool for better understanding force disengagement and confidence-building measures in specific regional security contexts. Output from the system could be tailored to meet the needs of individual end-users.

Conceptual Architecture of CMC

Figure 1 is a diagram of the conceptual architecture of the center. The far-left-hand column shows the wide range of possible input for the CMC: everything from purely technical sensor data to the text of regional agreements or confidence-building measures. A pre-processing unit shown in the next column would be necessary for performing functions such as image processing and sensor data processing and would provide input for the data fusion, analysis, and storage sub-system. Modeling and simulation could also provide input to the data fusion sub-system. The analysis performed under this sub-system would be aided by analytical tools tailored to the specific regional context. The output of the system would be customized to meet the needs of the user.

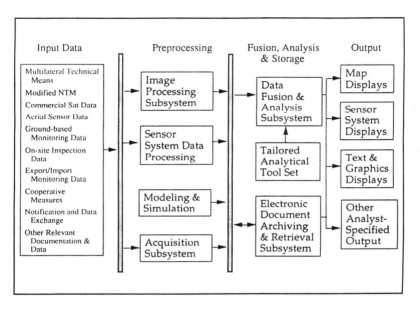

Input Data	Preprocessing	Fusion, Analysis & Storage	Output
Multilateral Technical Means Modified NTM Commercial Sat Data Aerial Sensor Data Ground-based Monitoring Data On-site Inspection Data Export/Import Monitoring Data Cooperative Measures Notification and Data Exchange Other Relevant Documentation & Data	Image Processing Subsystem Sensor System Data Processing Modeling & Simulation Acquisition Subsystem	Data Fusion & Analysis Subsystem Tailored Analytical Tool Set Electronic Document Archiving & Retrieval Subsystem	Map Displays Sensor System Displays Text & Graphics Displays Other Analyst-Specified Output

Figure 1: Conceptual Architecture of the Cooperative Monitoring Center (CMC).

The far-left-hand column shows the wide range of possible input for the CMC: everything from purely technical sensor data to the text of regional agreements or confidence-building measures. A pre-processing unit, shown in the next column would be necessary for performing functions such as image processing and sensor data processing and would provide input for the data fusion, analysis, and storage sub-system. Modeling and simulation could also provide input to the data fusion sub-system. Analysis would be aided by analytical tools tailored to the specific regional context. The output of the system would be customized to meet the needs of the user.

How the CMC Could Be Utilized

For example, consider a situation where the CMC is utilized to evaluate or experiment with a system to monitor compliance with an agreement to withdraw troops or equipment from a specified region. There are two ways the CMC could be utilized: first, to simulate the proposed agreement and monitoring scheme totally on the computer and, second, to try out the actual monitoring scheme in another physical location. In the first case, assume that the only allowed monitoring is satellite imagery. Input into the system would consist of three-dimensional maps of the region and a specified (time-dependent) configuration of military forces, including objects such as tanks; the ability to simulate the response of satellite sensors to the troop configuration would also be required. Analysts would use the system to evaluate the ability of satellites to monitor force withdrawal. They might come to the conclusion that satellites were insufficient in the particular geographical context and suggest additional sensors, such as ground-based seismic sensors or a more rigorous aerial overflight regime. These sensors could be included in the model to allow a second iteration.

The second case concerns a physical simulation where the user has the objective of getting experience with handling real sensor data concerning actual objects. Here, an experiment might be designed where tanks, or similar objects, were deployed in a geographical location bearing some qualitative resemblance to that in the Middle East region of concern. Input to the CMC could include commercial satellite imagery, aerial overflight data, and data from unattended ground sensors, along with maps containing the known tank configuration. The object of the analysis would be identification and location of tanks. An example of a tailored analytical tool is a target recognition algorithm that would allow automatic and rapid scanning of imagery and sensor data to perform such identification. The results of the image analysis could be represented on a three-dimensional map of the region to allow users to easily see the tank configuration at any time. Again, the synergistic effect of using other sensors could also be tested.

Modular Design Ensures Flexibility

Modularity would be designed into the monitoring center to ensure its flexibility. As shown in Figure 2, modules could consist of satellite, airborne, and ground-based sensors; in addition to a simulation module. The user could choose from a variety of sensors and sensor deployments from these modules, thereby creating customized systems for specific needs.

A satellite sensor module could utilize data from commercial satellites such as LANDSAT, SPOT, or ALMAZ, or commercial data from the GPS satellite system. Dedicated regional "light" satellites might also be feasible. These latter satellites could provide tracking capabilities and communication down-links as well as data from particular sensor platforms. Possible sensors include optical and thermal imaging sensors.

A concept for an airborne sensor module includes sensor platforms based on the Open Skies Treaty. Real-time communication down-links are also a possibility. Possible sensors include synthetic aperture radar, still and video optical sensors, thermal imaging sensors, air samplers, and electro-optical sensors. The ability to fly aircraft equipped with sensor platforms is included in the concept of the CMC.

A ground-based sensor module would include sensors such as infra-red and seismic detectors, video systems, and acoustic, magnetic, and weight detectors. Such sensors could be used alone or in combination with airborne or satellite sensors for a variety of applications from chokepoint monitoring to physical protection for high-value items or sites.

Integral to all sensor systems will be standard data security technologies such as tamper indication and data security

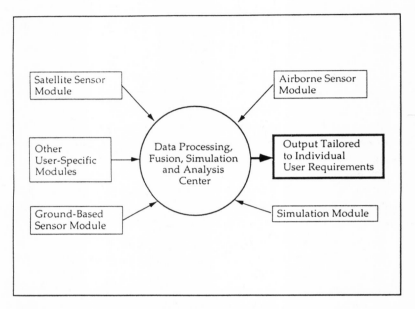

Figure 2: Modularity Increases the Flexibility of the Cooperative Monitoring Center.

Region-specific monitoring systems can be constructed by choosing from a variety of sensor and simulation modules.

capabilities. Familiarity with these concepts and processes is essential to the understanding of verification and monitoring capabilities.

The modeling and simulation module is conceived as having many capabilities, including scenario-specific sensor simulation for purposes of optimizing sensor deployment and synergy, and facility modeling to facilitate planning of on-site inspections. It may also be possible to develop methods to model force disengagement and the effects of implementation of agreements and confidence-building measures. Both physical and computer simulation methods are included in this concept.

TWO HYPOTHETICAL MONITORING SCENARIOS

Monitoring an Agreement to Restrict Tank Movements Near a Garrison

As part of an agreement to reduce force readiness and to limit troop deployment, assume that the sides have agreed to place all tanks in garrisons and to restrict tank movements to the garrison or its immediate vicinity. If a party to the agreement needs to move the tanks outside the designated range, for example, to take part in a military exercise, it is agreed that notification must be given in advance.

To monitor compliance with the agreement, each tank is equipped with an "electronic tag" that periodically signals its presence in the garrison. The signal is sent to a ground station and relayed to the other parties to the agreement via satellite (Figure 3). The electronic tag has a restricted range to match the terms of the agreement, and if the tank moves outside this range, the ground station will not receive its signal and the other parties to the agreement will be alerted to the possibility of noncompliance. The sides would have the opportunity to resolve the "suspicion" in a variety of ways. More intrusive monitoring

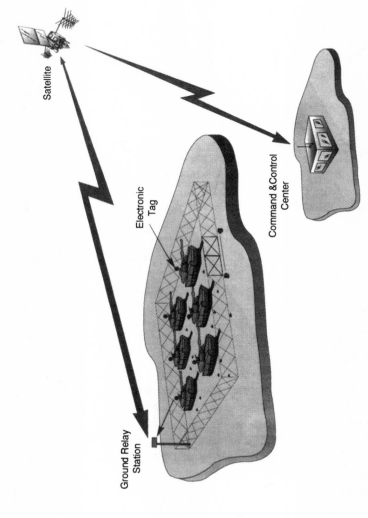

Satellite

Ground Relay
Station

Electronic
Tag

Command &Control
Center

Figure 3: A Hypothetical System to Monitor Compliance With an Agreement to
Restrict Tank Movement Near a Garrison.

could be triggered by the alert: for example, an aerial overflight of the suspected garrison or a visit by inspectors to check that all tags are functioning properly.

To preclude the possibility of moving tanks outside the garrison and falsely signaling their presence, each tag would include data-authentication technology that would match each signal with a particular tag. In addition, the tags would each incorporate tamper-indicating features that would transmit an alerting signal if the tag were tampered with. An agreed number of randomly timed overflights to count tanks might also provide the sides assurance that the system was accurately keeping track of the tanks.

Monitoring an Agreement To Not Move Troops Across a Bridge or Boundary

Assume that after implementation of an agreement to withdraw troops from a particular region, the sides wish to verify that troops are not clandestinely moved back in. If there is a chokepoint, such as a bridge or a mountain pass, through which equipment must cross, this chokepoint could be equipped with unattended ground sensors to verify that troops did not re-enter the region (Figure 4). If no human or vehicular traffic were allowed through the chokepoint, a variety of seismic sensors could be employed to detect movement and signal any detection. If the sides were only interested in movement of heavy objects, such as tanks, through the chokepoint, and were unconcerned with the movement of people and passenger vehicles, sensors that respond to weight, such as tilt-meters, could be utilized and set to signal an alert only if an agreed-upon high-weight threshold were exceeded. All sensors would include data security technology, as described previously. Again, if the unattended ground sensors signaled passage of heavy equipment, aerial overflights could be used to confirm the possibility of military redeployments.

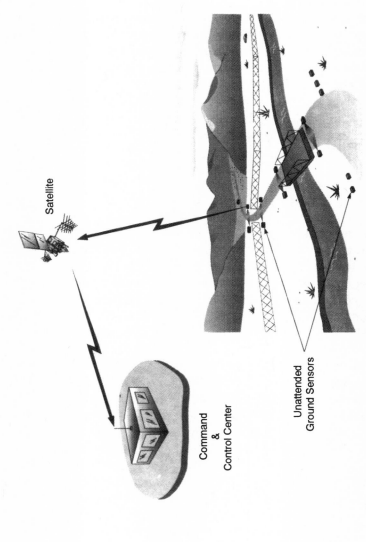

Satellite

Command & Control Center

Unattended Ground Sensors

Figure 4: A Hypothetical System to Monitor Compliance with an Agreement Not to Move Troops Across a Bridge or Boundary.

CONCLUSION

Verification and monitoring technologies can facilitate the pursuit of regional security in a variety of ways. During the negotiating process, communication between the technical and political communities is important for two reasons:

1. awareness of the capabilities of monitoring technology can influence the attitude of negotiators toward particular agreements and

2. knowledge about the specific issues involved in negotiations helps steer technology down relevant paths.

In this chapter, we have proposed a program to use technology to enhance the process of achieving peace in the Middle East.

Analysis of region-specific issues, such as possible confidence-building measures, and characterizing potential users of monitoring technologies will assure that proposed monitoring scenarios and technology systems are relevant and appropriate. This task can best be accomplished by a group composed of members of both the political and technical communities, including participants from the Middle East.

Demonstrations of systems of monitoring technologies, both within the region and in extra-regional neutral countries, can provide a means of communication between technology developers and its potential users. Such demonstrations would provide the basis for continuing interactions and collaborations, including joint research and development projects.

A Cooperative Monitoring Center would permit users from the region to experiment with monitoring hardware and data, computer simulations and modeling, data security technology, and information management and data fusion techniques. By providing access to satellite, airborne, and ground-based data and the associated data processing and analysis infrastructure, the center would function as a tool for evaluating monitoring requirements and designing monitoring systems for hypothetical or existing agreements.

ACKNOWLEDGMENTS

The authors are grateful to comments and critical review by Kent Biringer and Michael Vannoni of Sandia National Laboratories.

The Politics and Institutionalization of
Regional Security

10 The Multilateral Middle East Peace Talks: Reorganizing for Regional Security

Yezid Sayigh

The signing of the Palestinian–Israeli Declaration of Principles in Washington D.C. on 13 September, 1993, followed a day later by the signing of the Jordanian–Israeli Working Agenda, confirmed the extent to which the Middle East peace process has taken root, despite the initial reluctance of the parties and the fitful negotiations of the first two years. As the various parties build on these initial breakthroughs to conclude more detailed agreements that also include Syria and Lebanon, there is a growing need to look ahead to the regional security structures and cooperative arrangements that must be constructed in order to underpin the eventual peace treaties and to provide means for meeting the growing social, economic, and political challenges that confront the wider Middle East.

This chapter proposes the establishment of a region-wide agency that can help address the root causes of conflict, insecurity, and underdevelopment in the Middle East and so provide a means of moderating the destabilizing impact of external developments on the Arab–Israeli "security complex."

Such a "roof" organization could be based on the ongoing multilateral Middle East peace talks, in order both to seize the political opportunity they offer and build on their existing framework and to transform them into a more lasting vehicle for regional security and cooperation.

The assumption that breakthroughs in the bilateral talks effectively obviate the role originally envisaged for the multilaterals—to complement the bilateral talks and to build confidence and induce normal relations between the parties—would be erroneous. The regional dimension of peace and security is essential to the durability and stability of bilateral agreements, and it cannot depend indefinitely on the commitment of external, global powers. Rather, it must institutionalize the role of the regional actors themselves in a way that assigns them the primary responsibility for maintaining their own security and prosperity.

Of course, the Arab states and Israel (and other neighbors) are unlikely to start formal negotiations on the shape and purpose of a collective regional body, let alone establish one, before the main protagonists have concluded their final bilateral peace treaties. The interested parties in the Middle East itself and the international sponsors of the peace process should offer a practical vision, nonetheless, and should deliberately use the existing multilateral talks as a venue to discuss proposals and to set up some of the mechanisms that would eventually be brought together within an overarching regional organization.

The vision offered here centers on the establishment of a Multilateral Agency for Security and Cooperation in the Middle East (MASCME). The following sections examine the need for such a regional body and, by way of introduction, summarize the foreseeable threats to Middle East stability and the inadequacies of the multilateral talks as currently configured. Having expanded on the rationale for MASCME, subsequent sections of this chapter discuss its main aims, membership, organizational structure, operational scope, and practical functions.

IDENTIFYING THE NEED FOR A
MULTILATERAL AGENCY

Strategic Threats to Regional Stability

Anticipating the future security requirements of an Arab–Israeli peace is dictated, in part, by the complex nature of the Middle East "strategic system" and by the multiplicity of its actors and internal sources of conflict.[1] There is a high degree of political permeability and strategic vulnerability among the member-states in the system—the Arab countries, Israel, Iran and Turkey (some might add Afghanistan and Ethiopia)—for reasons of geography, history, society, and culture, giving rise to constant instability. The combination of social and political fragmentation enabled the main global powers to manipulate local conflicts to their advantage, as shown by the course of various conflicts in the Gulf, Horn of Africa, and Arab–Israeli "theaters" during the Cold War.

The overt, hostile East–West rivalry of the past may be over, but external powers will continue to play a heightened role throughout the region, especially given the proximity of southern Europe, the former Soviet republics, and South Asia, and, additionally, the global role and Cold War heritage that have introduced the U.S. as a key player in regional affairs. Indeed, the more recent Gulf War has created a remarkable, new status quo in which the U.S. both deploys its military might and exercises it actively within the region. The long-term implications of this unprecedented reality are not yet clear, but it at least suggests that the U.S. may be tempted to rely more on its own, direct presence, alliances, and global influence—in order to promote its vision of security, prosperity, and democracy—than on regional organizations.

The same factors (of geography, history, society and culture) also create numerous linkages throughout the Middle East, exposing the strategic balance in any of its subsidiary "security complexes" (or sub-regions)—such as the Gulf, Arab–Israeli arena, or Horn of Africa—to new pressures and threats whenever changes take place elsewhere in the wider system.[2] Such linkage drives, and in turn is driven by, a regional arms race that has developed an ominous momentum of its own.[3] In the course of the past few decades, the Middle East has witnessed the militarization of its societies and economies, acquisition of massive conventional weapons arsenals, proliferation of ballistic missiles and weapons of mass destruction, and growth of indigenous military R&D and production capabilities.[4]

There are, moreover, many current and foreseeable threats to regional stability. Relations between Iraq and its neighbors remain volatile, and the prospect of an Iraqi breakup and Kurdish independence can only disturb the balance of power and trigger a race for influence between Iraq, Iran, and Turkey (and, to a lesser extent, Syria and the Gulf Cooperation Council [GCC] states). The Iranian military reconstruction program alarms Saudi Arabia and other Arab states, especially as it may include an effort to develop ballistic missiles and a nuclear capability. Yet despite their concern and the momentous events of the Gulf crisis and war, strains among the GCC member-states impede its transformation into a viable collective security agency, while Saudi–Yemeni tensions may too eventually result in violence.

Further afield, the fate of the Western Sahara is once again poisoning Algerian–Moroccan relations and Libya is under international siege, while Islamist forces pose an increasing threat to government authority throughout North Africa and in Egypt. A confrontation has also built up between Egypt and the Islamist government in Khartoum, while to the south secessionism continues to wrack the Horn of Africa. On the other side of the Mediterranean, Balkan conflict threatens to activate Aegean tensions at a time when Turkey is adopting an increasingly assertive stance toward Syria and Iraq. Regional stability in the Middle East is also liable to be adversely affected, finally, by tensions between the former Soviet republics, infighting in Afghanistan, and Turkish–Iranian rivalry in Central Asia.

Non-Military Causes of Conflict

What makes the strategic dimension of regional security—that is, political and military security relations between states—especially unstable and resistant to conventional "management" is the emerging challenge to the Middle East system and its member states from within. State structures, national politics, societies, economies, and resource bases are undergoing a prolonged crisis at a time of momentous transition and readjustment in both the regional and international systems. The failures of the past, heavy external debts, and inability to meet the rapidly-growing demands of burgeoning, young populations pose a major challenge to most governments in the Middle East and threaten all its governments with continued instability. The race for resources, especially water, at a time of growing environmental degradation and declining financial power (due in part to the grim outlook for oil revenues and their reinvestment within the region) only accentuates the state of impending crisis as well as contributing to it at an increasing rate.[5]

A "lethal triangle" of challenges—structural, demographic, and resource/environmental—threatens a widening circle of Middle East states with political and economic crisis, if not collapse.[6] Evidence abounds: from Algeria in the Western Arab World, through Sudan and Somalia, to Lebanon and Iraq, past failures of ruling elites and their systems of power now raise serious questions about the territorial integrity of those countries and the ability of any new government to reestablish social harmony, political stability, and economic prosperity within the foreseeable future.

Challenges and material shortfalls have been kept in check elsewhere—in Egypt, Tunisia, Syria, Jordan, and Iran, for example—but at a high price. And unless political, economic, and administrative reforms are initiated, including a review or revival of legal systems, and external circumstances are favorable, providing needed infusions of political support and economic aid, management of stability will become increasingly difficult.

Even countries that are relatively wealthy and secure within their basic constituencies face narrowing options in reconciling the burden of meeting national priorities and policy objectives with the social and financial cost. Israel remains highly dependent on massive US aid and, until the Israeli–PLO agreement of September 1993, was well on the way to "internalizing" its conflict with the Palestinians. The Gulf Cooperation Council states are increasingly hard put to balance oil revenues with public expenditure, meanwhile, and face difficult choices between different defense policies with contrasting financial and social costs as well as renewed pressures for political liberalization.

An added threat is that these various crises and conflicts can, and will, come to affect inter-state relations in the Middle East within a few years. As discussed earlier, the modern history of state formation in the region, coupled with continuing social and political fragmentation and economic underdevelopment, have already made for a very close, almost symbiotic, relationship between and foreign policies since 1945. Several factors—the end of the Cold War, the dramatic demonstration of the new world and regional order offered by the second Gulf war, and the prospects of Arab–Israeli peace—make inter-state wars in the region unlikely for the rest of the 1990s, but the risk of a massive resurgence of regional upheaval cannot be precluded beyond the year 2000 if a growing circle of countries experience further decline or descend into open civil strife.

The factors of domestic change and conflict will simply not go away, and will increasingly dominate the Middle East strategic landscape in the next decade, at the very least. They will come increasingly to damage relations between states in the region and with the rest of the international community, as the prospect of turbulence and uncertainty provokes mutual hostility and deters the flow of aid, trade, and capital into the afflicted countries. The challenge facing regional states, with the constructive assistance of the global powers and international community, is at once to address the causes of conflict and to provide the context for stable interstate relations. In both cases best results can be achieved through collective organization and cooperative mechanisms.

Flaws in the Peace Process

The threats to peace and stability in the Middle East are obvious, making attainment of an Arab–Israeli peace in all its dimensions and the resolution of other regional problems imperative. Equally obvious is the need to underpin any Arab–Israeli settlement and safeguard it against future challenges. This is best achieved by constructing regional security structures that are capable of preempting the buildup of tensions, managing crises, and absorbing pressures generated by changes in the strategic environment.

However, the Middle East peace process as currently structured cannot fulfill the task. The bilateral talks launched in Madrid on 3 November, 1991, were designed to produce separate agreements between Israel and Syria, Lebanon, Jordan and the Palestinians, but lacked an overarching framework. Even if peace agreements are achieved, maintaining a stable strategic balance in the Arab–Israeli "security complex" in the future will depend entirely on a series of bilateral consultations and adjustments between Israel and each of its Arab counterparts. This places the main burden of regional security management on Israel, and, critics might charge, gives it undue ability to manipulate its neighbors to its advantage, provoking their resentment. It also makes instability an integral part of the strategic landscape. Each party will need to respond to inevitable changes in its external environment, but its responses might alarm its other neighbors and trigger countermoves, thus restarting the cycle of threat perception and conflict.

Nor can the multilateral talks launched in Moscow in late January 1992 resolve this problem. Their foremost aim was to reinforce the bilateral peace agreements between the direct "confrontation parties" by ensuring wider commitment to them in the region and in the international community, among Arab and non-Arab states. Achieving this aim would of course ease regional tensions and moderate their destabilizing impact on Arab–Israeli relations but could do so only partially at best, and indirectly at that.

This assessment is borne out upon examination of the five multilateral working groups that deal with wider regional concerns—arms control, economic development, water sharing, environmental challenges, and refugees. Although various practical proposals have been mooted, the approach remains piecemeal and disconnected—less than incremental, in fact—as much because of the preference and prejudice of the main cosponsor, the U.S., as because of resistance from the protagonists themselves.

The multilateral talks do not provide an institutionalized framework that can deal collectively with regional problems and causes of instability, since they will cease once the bilateral Arab–Israeli peace agreements are signed and sealed. There are no working groups on human rights and democratization, moreover, and so the multilateral forum offers no avenue for altering the political landscape in the Middle East in the long term, although that is the basis for lasting peace and security. Above all, the existing multilateral framework comes nowhere near anticipating, let alone addressing effectively, the depth and magnitude of the structural, social, economic and political crisis looming over the region. In brief, the shortcomings of the current Middle East peace process itself make it all the more necessary to anticipate the requirements of an Arab–Israeli peace at the regional level.

REORGANIZING FOR REGIONAL SECURITY

The Overall Framework

However carefully the various bilateral Arab–Israeli peace agreements are constructed, especially with regard to security, they will remain vulnerable to destabilization by events in the wider Middle East. The causes of conflict vary, and the pattern for the rest of the 1990s is increasingly toward civil strife rather than interstate war, but in all cases the prospects for upheaval and protracted conflict, of varying intensity, are strong. And, ultimately, internal strife can undermine the regional system of inter-state relations and threaten the fragile fabric of Arab–Israeli peace.

How then to provide a stable regional context for Arab–Israeli peace? The most obvious answer is to turn the current, loosely defined structure of the multilateral peace talks into a more clearly defined regional framework spanning the entire Middle East. This might be little more than a forum for open dialogue and discussion of matters of common concern, ranging from political and territorial disputes, through human rights and democratization, to issues of security and cooperation. Alternatively, it might seek to address the same concerns by evolving into a formal organization—a "roof" or "umbrella" body—with a more complex structure and practical functions.

This chapter specifically proposes the establishment of a Multilateral Agency for Security and Cooperation in the Middle East (MASCME). The central purpose is for regional actors to provide themselves with additional means for the prevention and management of crises, and even their resolution, and a way of complementing the work of smaller, sub-regional agencies, the U.N., and specialized international bodies working in various fields of arms control, economic development, and the environment, among others. In so doing, the MASCME would additionally help to stabilize the strategic environment of the Arab–Israeli security complex.

To a significant degree, the proposed MASCME resembles the Conference on Security and Cooperation in Europe (CSCE) in nature and purpose and should take it as a partial model. Of course, opponents of the CSCE will conclude the opposite: that the experience of Europe and the multiplicity of problems and actors plaguing the Middle East would render any similar organization useless, assuming it could be established at all. Critics consider the whole CSCE concept to be "woolly," with some justification, and patently unable to deal effectively with grave crises such as the violent breakup of Yugoslavia.

Nonetheless, the critics should pause to consider. The multilateral peace talks already form a collective, albeit loose, framework for Middle East peace, security and cooperation along the broad lines of the CSCE. The various working groups enjoy the support and active participation of the majority of regional and global powers that would be invited to assist a Helsinki-type process in the Middle East—the recalcitrant few still outside the talks might regard a formal regional agency with greater favor if they are reassured that it is responsive to their concerns and is not intended to isolate or exclude them.[7] Furthermore, as currently structured, the multilateral steering committee and separate working groups deal with distinct "baskets" of issues, similar to the setup within the CSCE. The ongoing multilateral peace talks focus on confidence-building, moreover, which was at the heart of the Helsinki process.

The organizational basis and political opportunity for a broadly similar approach in the Middle East already exist, therefore. Regardless of whether or not a Conference on Security and Cooperation in the Middle East (CSCME) is formally established, and whether or not it emerges in parallel to the multilateral peace talks or as their successor once an Arab–

Israeli peace is concluded, simply formulating the model will suggest ways of developing the current talks and help them reach a more successful and lasting conclusion.[8]

However, it is precisely because of the shortcomings and weaknesses of the CSCE model that this chapter suggests the establishment of a multilateral *agency*, rather than a conference, for security and cooperation in the Middle East. The implication is that an agency would have narrower, more practical functions, and would build more directly on the bodies and mechanisms being proposed within the ongoing multilateral Middle East peace talks. Its remit need not include negotiation of political relations between member states, at least initially, although this could be developed at a later stage.

Rather than act as a "talking shop," which is what some analysts consider the CSCE to be, the MASCME would act more as a "clearing house" and point of liaison between member states concerning issues of common concern. In this capacity, it would oversee the operation of subsidiary agencies and bodies dealing with those concerns at a practical level. The starting point would be the categories already adopted within the ongoing multilateral Middle East peace talks, although the range of specific functions and tasks should be revised and expanded fairly rapidly. Crucially, the MASCME would also contribute to crisis prevention, to the extent that it provides new, multiple channels for contact and agreed-upon norms and routines for behavior. As mutual confidence grows and regional states come to identify common political aims and values, moreover, the MASCME could go beyond the minimal level of crisis prevention to play a more direct, formal role in collective crisis management, conflict resolution, and arbitration in political and territorial disputes.

MEMBERSHIP AND FOUNDING PRINCIPLES

The MASCME would include all members of the Leagues of Arab States (including the Palestinians), as well as Israel, Iran, and Turkey. Ethiopia, Afghanistan, Malta, and—given its proximity and special security problems, arising from its partition and the presence of Turkish and British forces—Cyprus could also participate as observers, as might the Central Asian republics of the former USSR, depending on their status in collective agencies that might emerge in the future under Russian, Turkish, or Iranian auspices. The southern European countries could be invited as observers too, since they are Mediterranean littoral states, although full membership would be impeded by their role in NATO and the WEU.

In general, the fundamental criteria for inclusion would be geographical location and patterns of security relations, as well as shared concerns such as water, oil, or physical access (to waterways, for instance). Given their global role and close security relations with countries in the Middle East, the five permanent members of the United Nations Security Council would also be granted observer status in the MASCME. This would have the added advantage of involving the United Nations directly in the work of the MASCME; this U.N. role could then be replicated in the various subsidiary committees and agencies of the MASCME.

At the highest level, the MASCME would act as a multilateral forum covering the entire region, to discuss and agree shared guidelines on several "baskets" of issues, principally security, economic development, water and other natural resources, environment, political liberalization, and human rights (the latter category would subsume the issue of refugees). Membership in the Agency would depend on acceptance of certain basic principles such as the non-resolution of disputes by violence, respect for internationally recognized borders and the territorial integrity of states, inadmissibility of acquiring territory by force, non-intervention in the affairs of other states, and recognition of the equal rights and self-determination of peoples.[9]

Formal diplomatic recognition between members would not be a prerequisite for joining the MASCME, thus making it more acceptable to protagonists (although mutual recognition would occur once the bilateral peace agreements have been concluded). This would make it possible for non-state actors such as the PLO or Kurdish parties to attend as well as to seat Israel with its opponents if peace has not already been concluded. In all cases, however, MASCME members must be willing to endorse the preamble, based on such international documents as the U.N. Charter and Declaration of universal Human Rights, and on specific U.N. resolutions related directly to the region, such as Security Council Resolutions 242 and 338 (if not already implemented). With respect both to mutual recognition and the preamble, the MASCME would diverge from the example set by the European CSCE in order to adapt to local circumstances.

The Broad Agenda

Initially, the purpose of MASCME members would be to identify and agree the distinct categories—baskets—into which the main threats and concerns affecting the region can be divided. Each basket could then be discussed in greater detail by special committees, backed by technical sub-committees and specialized agencies as appropriate, composed of delegates representing those full members most interested. This structure would have the added advantage of allowing MASCME observers or even non-members to take active part, by including them in the debate on specific issues of concern to them within each committee or technical sub-committee. In adopting a more flexible notion of participation, the MASCME would again diverge from its European type-model and so adapt better to the greater diversity of countries, concerns, and cultures in the extended Middle East.

Indeed, the ability of the proposed MASCME framework to accommodate, and adapt to, the immense diversity of the region would be an important reason for establishing it. The varied nature of local conflicts might normally have made it difficult to engage a majority of the regional players, but the radical changes in the international balance of power since 1989 and the Gulf crisis and subsequent start of peace talks in the Middle East have created new opportunities that need to be seized without delay. Bringing two clearly-demarcated blocs into the Helsinki process and agreeing on a common agenda might appear simpler, in retrospect, but the CSCE was largely paralyzed until the revolution of 1989–1990 in East Europe transformed the strategic landscape. The Gulf crisis and war of 1991–1991 and the subsequent breakthroughs in the Arab–Israeli peace process in September 1993 have ushered in the start of a similar, radical restructuring of the strategic landscape in the Middle East. At the same time, the need there for a Helsinki-style confidence-building process is made even more urgent precisely because there are several active, ongoing conflicts and impending crises over access and resources in the region.

Diversity could prove beneficial in the Middle East, in further contrast to the European experience, partly by preempting the emergence of monolithic blocs with single-track agendas.[10] At the very least, the cumulative contribution that was made over two decades by the protracted, incremental debate within the CSCE may be replicated in the Middle East. More hopefully still, the MASCME could prove instrumental in providing the very region-wide forum for common debate and even conflict resolution that has been so lacking there in the past. In doing so, it would constrain the stronger or richer states of the Middle East to some degree, and by the same token afford the weaker or poorer states added protection. While this broad, political debate is evolving, however, the MASCME would make its main contribution by focusing on the practical measures and issues that can help prevent conflict and increase cooperation.

The Srategic Dimension

The most obvious and immediate area of common concern is how to prevent or control armed conflict. Whether to reinforce Arab–Israeli peace or contain the arms race elsewhere in the Middle East, the MASCME basket dealing with security and arms control would be of special importance. It would provide a valuable forum for discussing military issues that have a regional impact, foremost of which is the proliferation of weapons of mass destruction. Rather than deal with the problem solely in global terms—at the United Nations, through talks on the Chemical and Biological Weapons Conventions, or in discussing an updated Nuclear Non-Proliferation Treaty—or regard it as a sticking point in face-to-face bilateral negotiations, the various Middle East parties could additionally use the MASCME to formulate guidelines adapted to local circumstances.

This would be of special value in reinforcing agreements concluded in the Arab–Israeli context regarding non-conventional weapons, the conventional arms race, indigenous military research, development, and production, and the use of space. Once peace agreements have been concluded between Israel and its immediate neighbors, moreover, there will be a real need to provide the means to absorb and counter the destabilizing effect that future changes in military capability or strategic posture elsewhere in the Middle East may have on the Arab–Israeli "complex." A case in point is the potential impact of Iranian conventional rearmament and non-conventional weapons programs, that would prompt Iraqi and Saudi Arabian counter-buildups, in turn seen as threatening by Israel and as destabilizing its relations with its Arab neighbors. Others are the emergence of advanced conventional munitions and force restructuring, both of which could significantly improve military capabilities.

The MASCME would fulfill two functions in the security sphere. On the one hand, it would allow individual states or sub-regional blocs to engage parties in other "security complexes" in the Middle East with which they might not normally be in contact in order to discuss issues of common concern. The size of the group would be smaller than international bodies such as the U.N. Disarmament Agency, making the discussion more manageable and allowing better focus on practical solutions. This, in turn, would conceivably allow MASCME members to make a more meaningful and effective contribution to global negotiations on the same issues. It would also enable them to discuss policy directions with extra-regional powers—primarily the nuclear and chemical materials and technologies supplying members of the London Club, Australia Group, Missile Technology Control Regime, and so on—in a way that places the concerns and priorities of Middle East parties more firmly on the international agenda. The MASCME could run its own local "chapters" or versions of those supplier control agencies.

On the other hand, once measures had been agreed upon or an Arab–Israeli peace concluded, the MASCME framework could take over supervision of Arab–Israeli security arrangements and help revise them (when made necessary by political or technological developments). In particular, it could oversee creation of a Middle East Nuclear-Biological-Chemical (NBC) weapons free zone, organize inspection and verification modalities, and establish information collection and distribution centers. The same forum could adopt general guidelines on the uses of space, both for monitoring and for non-military purposes, and present a local counterpart in the interpretation and implementation of measures designed to curb the conventional arms race, such as the U.N. international register.

In fact, this monitoring role would be one of the chief functions of the MASCME (in all baskets, not only in security).

Regional Non-military Cooperation

The other main function of the MASCME would be to develop those dimensions that underlie (or undermine) security, in the deeper, broader sense of the word. Security, whether internal or external; national or regional, is an integral concept based on political, economic and social components; scarcity of resources, such as water, or environmental problems, can be as threatening to real security as military challenges.[11] There can be little doubt that resolution of the Palestine and Arab–Israeli conflicts depends on a combination of political and territorial concessions and military arrangements, but addressing the other causes of instability in the region would weaken the agents of renewed conflict and offer incentives for growing regional cooperation.

The MASCME agenda in the non-military spheres should expand and diversify with time but would initially include the main headings already addressed by the multilateral Middle East peace talks with some modification. The Agency could quickly gain a practical economic function, for example, by overseeing the establishment of a regional reconstruction and development bank. As the experience of more successful regional organizations such as ASEAN shows, moreover, an initial focus on the common economic agenda can be a viable basis for better political and security relations. Looking at the relatively poor record of economic cooperation and trade within the Middle East—especially when oil exports are excluded—the MASCME could also complement the role of U.N. and other international agencies by raising the incentives; this could be achieved in part by discussing ways of facilitating intra-regional exchanges, through reforming customs and trade laws, and by targeting communications and transport for development.

Another function of the MASCME would be to oversee the establishment and operation of a regional environmental agency that could debate the use of water, power, and natural resources as well as deal with more direct problems of the environment. As in the case of economic development, the agency and its subordinate bodies would also play the part of a "clearing house" for information and of a center for liaison and crisis prevention. It would also observe implementation of protocols agreed by members concerning the use of water or environmental protection, among other matters. In this sense, as in others, the MASCME would tend to replicate the role of larger international organizations, but by limiting its membership and narrowing its focus to the Middle East, it could prove to be a more effective mechanism for quantifying problems and implementing general guidelines.

The MASCME could and should seek to expand its brief and strengthen peace by diversifying and multiplying the functional areas in which it promotes regional cooperation. Initially at least, it could focus on matters related to the security sphere or deriving from them. A case in point is the possibility of working from agreements on aerial inspection or naval accident management to negotiate free civilian use of air and sea routes—a civilian version of Open Skies and Open Seas. Training personnel to perform these various tasks would itself be another contribution of the Agency. The need for greater transparency regarding arms transfers and production should be extended to include defense budgets, paving the way for greater budget transparency generally; this would improve use of development aid and allow better use of economic incentives to promote arms control, human rights, and environmental responsibility.

Evidently, the most difficult aspect of the MASCME agenda to pursue is the broad basket of human rights, refugees, and political liberalization issues. This is likely to arouse the most resistance among local states, and poses the greatest conceptual obstacles to agreeing shared norms and standards, let alone agreed-upon rules of behavior and mechanisms for collective action. Yet progress in this sphere is pivotal for the long-term stability of regional peace and security. The MASCME must therefore confirm general acceptance of certain basic principles enshrined in the U.N. Charter and elsewhere and form a select number of watchdog agencies to monitor adherence to fundamental norms.

The MASCME is unlikely to achieve much progress in the political and human rights sphere even so and might usefully adopt an indirect approach to attain results, however modest, in the medium and long term. This would be to engage members in discussion of legislative and administrative reforms that are necessary for economic reform and development and that, in turn, make political liberalization both necessary and attractive. A special sub-agency could assist this process and help identify appropriate approaches by directing aid to non-governmental organizations, community projects, and self-help income-generating projects or other grassroots schemes as part of the economic development and environmental protection programs. In each case, the idea would be to find means of nudging local governments toward compliance without confrontation through practical, incremental means.

CONCLUSION: TURNING VISION INTO REALITY

It may be that the global powers, and particularly the U.S., believe that they can suffice with a minimalist, "crisis management" approach to the region and its problems. That is, they may hope to stabilize the current, post-Gulf war *status quo*, reinforcing it through the bilateral security relations they maintain with key allies, rather than rely on creating or strengthening local collective security agencies. Yet this would simply perpetuate the policies of the Cold War, when U.S.– Soviet and Arab–Israeli polarization made conflict-resolution impracticable and the formation of collective security pacts or regimes unthinkable. Worse still, crisis management was designed primarily to head off conflict once it had become imminent or control it after it had begun rather than *prevent* it altogether, which is a crucial requirement for the future of Arab–Israeli peace.

Old habits die hard, but it would be a pity to miss the opportunities offered by the end of the Cold War and the imminent resolution of the Arab–Israeli conflict to develop new approaches and new policies for the Middle East. Indeed, it would be more than a pity, it would be dangerous. As the Iraqi invasion of Kuwait showed most graphically, policies based on crisis management and bilateral alliances are helpless to preempt threats or prevent conflict in moments of major regional or international transition. Many such moments are on the way in the Middle East and its environs, and so to rely on such an approach in the Arab–Israeli "security complex" would be fraught with the risk of renewed conflagration.

Conversely, by setting the Arab–Israeli peace talks in wider scope and offering a vision of what the final settlement might look like, it becomes easier to persuade the negotiators to make necessary concessions and to accept certain asymmetries, because they are assured of an exchange and that their core claims and concerns will still be addressed. Indeed, this elaboration of a final "package deal"—embodied in the MASCME—forms the conceptual link that is so far missing between the current agendas for the multilateral and bilateral peace talks. Trade-offs are the key to successful negotiations, but without a sense of the wider context or its linkages and an assurance of mutuality and reciprocity, willing compromise becomes impossible and lasting peace unattainable.

It may not yet be possible to commence negotiation on the actual establishment of a MASCME, nor is it intended to replace the current multilateral talks, but more of its likely principles, policies, and institutions should be developed within the existing forum as a means of bringing it about. The ongoing multilateral talks can be used to acclimatize the parties—through cooperation on modest, technical issues and on institutionalization of lesser confidence-building measures—to the eventual establishment of a formal regional organization once the various bilateral agreements have resolved outstanding disputes and laid the basis for a comprehensive Arab–Israeli peace.

A historic "window of opportunity" to establish peace and security for all in the Middle East exists, opened by the dramatic changes in the USSR and East Europe since 1989 and the Gulf conflict of 1990–1991. It offers a chance to make an evolutionary step forward in the approach of the international community to global security, not only from balance of power thinking to collective security but a step further toward cooperative security. The Palestinian–Israeli Declaration of Principles and the Jordanian–Israeli Working Agenda of September, 1993 represent a modest, but significant step through that "window," not least because the language and spirit of mutual security and cooperation suffused both texts. The opportunity cannot last indefinitely and must be seized in order to achieve a comprehensive Arab–Israeli settlement and create effective regional agencies. Otherwise, the Middle East will emerge from the momentous transition that the international system is undergoing to suffer further bloodshed and impoverishment.

NOTES

1. The notion of the Arab states as a strategic system is developed in Paul Noble, "The Arab State System: Pressures, Constraints and Opportunities," in Bahgat Korany and Ali Dessouki, eds., *The Foreign Policies of Arab States* (Boulder and London: Westview Press and Cairo: American University in Cairo Press, 1991) (revised edition).

2. The notion of the "security complex" is developed by Barry Buzan in "The Future of the South Asian Security Complex," in Barry Buzan and Gowher Rizvi et al., *South Asian Insecurity and the Great Powers* (London: Macmillan, 1986).

3. The complexity of the Middle East strategic system, its linkages, and the destabilizing impact of nonconventional weapons proliferation are discussed in Yezid Sayigh, "Middle East Stability: The Impact of the Proliferation of Weapons of Mass Destruction," in Ephraim Karsh, Martin Navias, and Philip Sabin, eds., *Non-Conventional Weapons Proliferation in the Middle East* (Oxford: Oxford University Press, 1993), pp. 179–203.

4. A summary of the regional arms trade since the beginning of the 1970s is in Yezid Sayigh, *Arab Military Industry: Capability, Performance and Impact* (London: Brassey's, 1992), ch. 2–3.

5. One author (Natasha Beschorner) argues that water rivalries will not lead to outright conflict.

6. "Structural" crisis refers to the decreasing ability of state structures to cope with or provide for the needs of growing populations, and to the wider problem of institution-building in both the public and private sectors.

7. The cases of Iraq, Iran, Libya, and Sudan offer an excellent example of the contrast between approaches. While the policy urged by some within the Clinton administration is based on "outlawing" these countries, for example under the notion of "dual containment" proposed by National Security Council advisor and former pro-Israeli lobbyist Martin Indyk, a more rational approach would be to seek ways of encouraging those countries to reintegrate within the regional system. One way to do so is to establish channels for dialogue and institutional fora for discussion of mutual concerns.

8. A cogent argument for the formation of a CSCME is presented by Tim Niblock, "The Realms Within Which Regional Co-operation and Integration Could be Fostered," in Gerd Nonneman, ed., *The Middle East and Europe: An Integrated Communities Approach* (London: Federal Trust, 1992), pp. 45–49.

9. Taken from the Helsinki Final Act, Helsinki, August 1, 1975. Department of State Publication No. 8826 (General Foreign Service No. 298), brought in R. Falk, B. Weston, A. D'Avanto, *Basic Documents in International Law and World Order* (St. Paul, MN: West Publishing Co., American Casebook Series, 1990) (2nd ed.), pp. 114–20.

10. The similarities and differences between the CSCE and proposed MASCME are obvious when comparing some of the basic principles and mechanisms. For a detailed study of the former, see, for example, V. Mastny, ed., *Helsinki, Human Rights, and European Security* (Raleigh, NC: Duke University Press, 1986).

11. For a fuller discussion of this definition of security, see Yezid Sayigh, *Confronting the 1990s: Security in the Developing Countries* (London: Brassey's for the International Institute for Strategic Studies, 1990).

11 Modalities and Sequences in the Multilateral Arms Control Talks in the Middle East

Etel Solingen

INTRODUCTION

It is no small paradox that Middle Eastern countries are busily engaged in designing a more promising regional future in the midst of otherwise chaotic developments in the emerging new world order, from national disintegration to proliferation of weapons of mass destruction. For most of the Cold War era, the Middle East engendered threats to global and regional security. Today, notwithstanding rugged interludes, negotiations for a comprehensive Arab–Israeli peace are a relatively bright spot in a sea of pressing concerns for international peace and stability.

The first part of this chapter examines the background conditions that made the current Middle East arms control negotiations possible. It then reviews the role of confidence-building measures (CBMs) in the early stages of arms control negotiations. It goes on to emphasize the advantages of a strategy of *sequencing*: 1) for dealing with states that have not yet joined in the multilateral peace talks and 2) for securing support for arms control and the peace process as a whole. The chapter ends with some recommendations specifically geared to strengthen political support for arms control and for a comprehensive peace settlement among countries in the region.

GENERAL BACKGROUND: THE ROAD TO THE MULTILATERAL PEACE TALKS

Current arms control negotiations in the Middle East—and the broader peace process of which it is a part—are the outcome of political change at the global, regional, and local levels. The demise of the Soviet Union and the outcome of the Gulf War rearranged the strategies of countries in the region and offered the United States a unique opportunity to become the midwife of the 1991 Madrid Conference—the birthplace of all ongoing peace negotiations, in the bilateral and multilateral contexts. The emerging consensus over economic and political liberalization and the defeat of its ideological nemeses—the Soviet Union, Iraq, and others—strengthened political forces sympathetic to the new order. Enough domestic support could now be marshaled throughout most countries in the region for the idea of a comprehensive settlement of the Arab–Israeli conflict. Lagging progress in the context of the Madrid process opened the way to a more dramatic step negotiated in a sheltered Norwegian environment: the September 1993 Declaration of Principles between Israel and the PLO.

Interlocutors to the multilateral peace negotiations share a fundamental political strategy that ties their own political health to regional and international cooperation. The common denominator among the PLO, King Hussein, President Mubarak, and Israel's Labor-led coalition is their expectation of positive economic and political windfalls from a peace settlement. The promise of replacing a huge military burden with a developmental bonanza and greater international competitiveness requires mutual concessions. Such concessions might seem politically risky in the short term but hold great potential for decimating the ranks of political rivals at home. In other words, the success of this strategy may not only benefit the citizens of this region but the political leadership embracing a "trading state" approach as well.[1]

Political groups throughout the region challenging the coalitions pursuing a regional settlement span the ideological spectrum, from radical fundamentalists to remnants of Cold War-era nationalists.[2] They do, however, share a political strategy. For the most part, they include movements advancing confessional causes, religious or nationalist, both in Israel and the Arab world. Very often these groups reject the practical and normative implications of integrating their countries politically and economically with what they regard as a "Western" world order. These groups oppose a regional settlement of the Arab–Israeli conflict because a settlement devoids them of a large share of their political capital. Where this coalition has prevailed politically, as in Iran, Iraq, and Sudan, the prospects of these states' joining the multilateral peace process seem largely doomed.[3]

SEQUENTIAL ASPECTS OF REGIONAL ARMS CONTROL

The agenda for arms control negotiations is indeed a bulky one, ranging from relatively minor technical measures to reduce the likelihood of accidents or misperceptions to securing a zone free of weapons of mass destruction.[4] The successful completion of an agreement requires a clever design of the sequence within which different issues might be addressed.

First, a consensus among the parties seems to be emerging with respect to one type of sequence: a comprehensive *political* settlement must *precede* any far-ranging *military* agreement. The September 1993 Declaration of Principles, and the *de facto* endorsement of an eventual two-state solution by Israel and the

PLO, bode well for the prospects that the core political issues at stake might be resolved, opening the way for a broader regional settlement.

Second, there is also a measure of consensus on the sequencing of steps internal to the process of arms control. For instance, the value of identifying mutually acceptable confidence- and security-building measures (CSBMs)—as a first step to break through the toughest initial phases of negotiating over security matters—is clear to all. The preferred sequence in the realm of CSBMs is one that begins with declaratory principles and steps to increase trust in the adversary's intentions and ends with measures that reduce actual military capabilities. In other words, this sequence progresses from "software" (for instance, doctrines, notification of military exercises) to "hardware" (force reductions, elimination of weapon systems), both of which assume measures that improve communication and transparency. The sequence involves steps to prevent accidents and unintended threats; such steps do not undermine but strengthen the individual security of the parties.

Third, in contrast to a convergence around the first two aspects of sequencing, strong disagreement exists with regards to sequencing negotiations over conventional versus non-conventional weapons. The Arab parties, under strong leadership of Egypt on this particular issue, place Israel's presumed nuclear capabilities and accession of all parties to the NPT at the top of the agenda.[5] Israel prefers to deal with what it considers the ultimate insurance policy for its existence, at the very end of the process, once cooperation has become more of an habit than an anomaly.[6]

It is often argued that the Arab position reveals little understanding of Israel's existential fears. In reality, the position adopted by the Arab parties does not exclude the possibility that they understand Israel's threat perceptions all too well but that they prefer to ignore them for one of two reasons.

First, Egyptian leaders express publicly a concern with the implications of an unrestrained non-conventional Israeli capability for the ability to curtail nuclear programs in countries like Iran and Algeria. Yet the idea that binding Israel will pave the way to disarm others is no more than a premise and perhaps one too risky to consider from the perspective of *all* partners to the multilateral talks. Consider the comments of Ayatollah Mohammed Beheshti, a close advisor to Khomeini, urging an Iranian scientist: "It is your duty to build the atomic bomb for the Islamic Republican Party"[7] or President Rafsanjani's deputy, Ataollah Mohajerani, declaring that "the entirety of Muslim states" should be equipped with a nuclear capacity."[8] The idea of an Islamic bomb may well be in the realm of "myth building,"[9] but these statements leave little doubt as to the intentions of powerful elements in the Iranian leadership.

A second consideration underpinning Arab governments' demand for early attention to nuclear matters may be related to an attempt to seek the kind of concessions that these governments believe might provide them with the highest political returns at home. Nurturing support for international agreements is part and parcel of the bargaining process for all parties.[10] Israeli leaders face serious internal constraints in that, at least in the public perception, Israel is the only party divesting itself of actual security assets (primarily territory). Public opinion polls suggest that any government asking Israelis to give up—in the same breath—the Golan Heights, most of the West Bank, and the ambiguous but reassuring strategic deterrent, will simply not survive. The prospects of a Labor defeat—and of a Likud comeback—might be frightful not only for the future of Israel but for Labor's Arab partners in the peace process as well.

Not enough is known, at least in the public domain, about the internal political process in Arab countries that fuels a demand for immediate consideration of the nuclear issue. Different prescriptions would stem from a situation where the military establishment is the major constituency on this issue than from a situation where broader popular demands compel a rigid enforcement of that negotiating posture. The popular literature and Arab press seem to be consistent in placing the solution of the Palestinian problem at the top of the agenda, and it took a Labor-led government in Israel to reach this historic compromise (still in the making) on this issue. Instead, the nuclear issue is far more symbolic from an Arab standpoint; the argument that Israeli capabilities are anything other than defensive is not taken seriously even by those in the international community who work assiduously to denuclearize the region.[11] Thus, there may be more effective payoffs from tackling first the *real* threat (for all sides) from a conventional attack and then moving on to far more *remote* (unreal, some would argue) dangers. As Yezid Sayigh, coordinator of the Palestinian team to the Multilateral Working Group on Arms Control, suggests: "Nuclear disarmament and the establishment of a nuclear-weapon-free zone could be delayed until the conventional threat was removed."[12] Such concessions on the Arab side would, of course, need to be reciprocated in other areas.

In the end, there is no better alternative for the region as a whole than the creation of a stable zone free of weapons of mass destruction. As to the modalities for verifying such a zone, it is interesting to consider for a moment the Brazilian–Argentine agreements of 1991 and the ensuing process of denuclearization of the region. The initial sequence agreed upon by both parties involved mutual inspections, to be complemented by trilateral arrangements with the IAEA. This provides an interesting precedent for the Middle East. It is sometimes asserted that the two regions are not comparable in light of the differing levels of effective security threats in which they are enmeshed. Paradoxically, however, it may be argued that precisely where levels of threat are lower one might have expected greater reliance on purely multilateral means of inspection and verification (which are often considered less reliable than bilateral ones). Yet, the fact that bilateral mutual mechanisms were embraced at the outset even in the southern cone of Latin America strengthens the case of those who would like to see them adopted in the Middle East as well. At the same time, all parties should recognize the need to involve international organizations in a supportive capacity.

IMPLICATIONS AND ADVANTAGES OF SEQUENCING

A strategy of sequencing ties arms control negotiations to the political process, both at the regional level, and at the level of domestic politics. It thus prevents the negotiations from proceeding at an unreal pace or being deprived of the benefits of trade-offs and linkages that the bilateral and multilateral contexts offer. Two important implications of sequencing are worth exploring in some detail:

a. The question of "outsiders," or states not yet parties to the multilateral talks and movements who feed on the opposition to them.

Syria, Lebanon, Libya, Iraq, and Iran are not part of the multilateral peace process and all host the most recalcitrant elements opposed to it (including Hezbollah, the Popular Front for the Liberation of Palestine [PFLP], and the Democratic Front for the Liberation of Palestine [DFLP], among others). From the standpoint of these "outsiders," an agreement among "insiders" over CBMs points to an emerging *entente* among participants in the arms control process, suggesting that negotiations are for real, even if they do not crack—at the outset—the toughest issues. The more effective the CBMs agreed upon, the higher the likelihood that they will induce anxiety among those who have left themselves out of the process. Even the implementation of a Red Sea communications and crisis prevention center that excludes Syria, Iran, and Iraq will provide a clear signal to non-participants that the costs of remaining aloof may increase rather than decrease.

These costs can serve as useful ammunition for supporters of reform within countries like Iran and Syria. The "economy first" wing of the Islamic Republic of Iran favors a policy geared to liberalize the economy, increase trade and foreign investments, and adopt a utilitarian—as opposed to an ideological—foreign policy.[13] Participation in a regional security framework would undermine efforts by radical leaders at home to blow Iran's "security dilemma" out of proportion and would free resources to undertake the economic reconstruction that pragmatists consider inevitable to prevent a collapse of the Islamic regime. In Syria, the more the country excludes itself from progress made by other Middle East partners, the more the regime distances itself also from its primary objective: its own political survival through economic reform.[14] This is so because the benefits of economic exchange will not, in all likelihood, accrue to Syria unless and until it becomes an effective partaker in a regional political *and military* settlement. Important elements of Assad's domestic coalition, such as the business community, may find their gains from economic liberalization to be far lower than they might be under a genuine transformation of the country's political economy.[15] The regime's temptation to bow to old patterns of military consumption of expenditures is a major bottleneck in this transformation.

At the same time, the very fact that partners to the arms control negotiations proceed sequentially—from the least to the most substantive aspects of military capabilities—reminds "outsiders" that the cooperative realm emerging among "insiders" does not diminish the latter's individual ability to inflict heavy penalties in response to unprovoked threats by third parties.

b. The question of building domestic popular confidence in CSBMs and the arms control process as a whole.

Political considerations often take second place in the context of arms control negotiations, perhaps because these negotiations are largely managed by highly technical (often military) experts, more concerned with substance than with the nitty-gritty aspects of the political process. Yet, ratification of the ultimate agreement is crucial, even when such ratification comes about through different institutional and procedural means in every country. The assumption that arms control may be the one issue (out of five in the multilateral process) that is most removed from public scrutiny is certainly false with respect to Israel, and perhaps with respect to highly vulnerable Arab states—such as Jordan—as well. What are the advantages of sequencing for building public support for the arms control negotiations?

Sequencing is essential to instill confidence in a process perceived to involve a progressive shedding of strategic endowments (mostly in the case of Israel) and of obsolete political objectives (in the case of Arab countries). Political leaders can use this parceling of consecutive reciprocal steps to build down security concerns at the popular level. The "security dilemma" is not merely a product of geostrategic conditions. Leaders can choose to fuel the dilemma (by exacerbating perceptions of the other side's offensive intentions) to serve their own political purposes, or they can help ameliorate the dilemma (by pointing to positive changes in the adversary's positions). The first path is far too often assumed to involve high political payoffs. The second path requires leadership and, in the end, may be no less, and perhaps far more rewarding politically. This path involves an effective campaign of educating the public. As Harkabi argues "in democratic regimes an island of wisdom can no longer last if surrounded by an ocean of stupidity."[16] This principle applies not only to Israel but also to states at various stages of democratization, where progressive civic inclusion can have a dramatic effect on a state's proclivity to embrace war or peace.

Sequencing thus ensures that agreements that may be arrived at in the context of arms control negotiations are not invalidated by political realities at home. Such realities in Israel include majority (two-thirds) support for taking security risks that may lead to a mutually beneficial political settlement;[17] however, as I discussed earlier, it also includes widespread concerns with physical survival. The unprovoked Iraqi SCUD missile attacks in 1991 have only reinforced such concerns.[18] Israeli leaders thus feel compelled to retain a policy of nuclear ambiguity until deep structural changes in intentions and capabilities have taken place in the region. Providing an insurance policy against "times of gloom"[19] makes other—more immediate—concessions more palatable. Such concessions could run the range of issue areas affected by the multilateral talks, from water to economic development.

It is far more complex to assess the sequence of arms control moves acceptable from the vantage point of political realities in the Arab world. Not every Arab party to the multilateral arms control negotiations faces the same internal threats or ranks threats equally. Yet, there seems to be a common theme in the political predicament of Arab leaders negotiating regional peace. Israeli occupation of the West Bank and Gaza, and its eventual demise, is at the heart of Palestinian concerns; Palestinians are the one party with least reason to fear Israel's non-conventional capabilities, by virtue of its physical presence in the midst of the Israeli state. The PLO might be far better positioned to face Hamas's challenges by delivering *first* on statehood and reconstruction and only later on purely symbolic issues. Similarly, Jordanian and Egyptian leaders stand a far better chance of handling discontent with the peace process through immediate and tangible resources to tackle their agonizing economic problems than with intangible gains with little operative meaning for the lives of the average citizen.

Sequencing may thus provide all current leaders in the region with the opportunity to abrogate, in an incremental way, many old slogans used in the past to coalesce political support. Yehoshafat Harkabi rightly argued that the Arab–Israeli conflict as a whole can hardly be reduced to a problem of misperceptions,[20] and misperceptions do not seem to be a genuine feature of formal negotiations today. At the same time, in the past political leaders in the region—in the expectation of political gains—have often exacerbated misperceptions at the popular level. Because the public is often less proficient in the details, it is susceptible to becoming a consumer of distorted characterizations of the adversary and of its own side's virtues as well. It is up to responsible leaders to re-educate their citizens to shed old habits. More practically, it may be politically untenable for current ruling coalitions to pursue the peace process without embracing that educational task. Instead, appeasing combative elements in their midst might look cost-effective in the short term, but could risk the longer-term objectives of economic and social reconstruction in the region. In sum, sequencing can help leaders deliver some immediate benefits while guiding, rather than following, the transformation of the political spectrum. Specifying the opportunity costs of failing to reach an agreement may help enlist the "median voter's" support for concessions.

On the one hand, Israelis will be asked to make very significant concessions at the bilateral and multilateral negotiating tables, particularly on territories (West Bank and Golan Heights), water, the environment, and refugees. Even in the more variable-sum game of economic exchange, Israel might have to subsume certain security risks to the prospects of overall economic benefits for all. The heavy task confronting the Israeli government is thus to build support for such concessions, including risky ones, that stop short of endangering the survival of the state. So far, Labor and Meretz's more moderate definition of such survival thresholds have fared well politically, despite growing concern with difficulties in the implementation of the Declaration of Principles.

On the other hand, the more Arab leaders can point to substantive progress on Palestinian existential issues (self-determination, statehood, personal and collective security) the better equipped they will be to buttress support for an arms control sequence that takes into account Israeli existential fears (physical survival). It is important to bear in mind that Arab leaders would only be promoting acceptance of the idea of *sequencing*, not of recognizing Israel's unilateral right to a nuclear deterrent for the remainder of history. The ultimate outcome—a zone free of weapons of mass destruction—fulfills the criteria of equity which Arab governments rightfully believe to be a political requirement for any stable agreement.

CONCLUSIONS AND RECOMMENDATIONS

Multilateral negotiations on arms control ought to be sensitive to political considerations: one's own and those of the adversary as well. This point may seem quite trite; yet, negotiations often take on a life of their own, where the internal logic of arms control prevails over the external logic of the political context. The difficulties in arriving at a consensus on the appropriate conventional–non-conventional arms sequence seem to be an example of such pitfalls.

Concessions in the area of arms control can be made more palatable by highlighting the potential gains in this and other issue areas under discussion in the multilateral negotiations. This course may have been underused so far. Negotiators to the arms control talks might, for instance, organize a special workshop on the expected benefits (particularly economic) of alternative frameworks of demilitarizing the region. This would not require a specific commitment to any particular framework. It would, instead, provide a more tangible essence of the public benefits that would accrue from mutual concessions. For instance, agreements on limiting a certain weapon system or reducing force structures can be translated into the actual size of saved expenditures. Proceedings from the workshop could be summarized in a document that, although not intrinsically binding for the purpose of actual negotiations, may elicit increased political support and public awareness of the peace dividends from mutual concessions.

All partners may also consider the possibility of defining self-binding commitments in the arms control area (e.g., renouncing the threat or use of force for political purposes or as an instrument of changing territorial borders). Such commitments may accomplish a number of objectives, at home and abroad. In the first place, they may be seen as a concrete show of political leadership. They would also fulfill the educational task facing all leaders in the region. Moreover, self-binding commitments can increase credibility in the eyes of interlocutors to the peace negotiations.[21] They also tend to elicit international support (moral and material) for the committing party. Ultimately, such commitments entail high value as a tool to bind the public to a given position, akin to making the public something of a partner at the table. The decisions by the PLO and Israel's Labor–Meretz coalition to negotiate directly with each other had these effects. Reverting a commitment that generates such positive international reverberations entails high costs, as the negotiating partners are all too aware. In the past, political leaders in the region were mostly concerned with the effects of failure in *war*-making (i.e., defeat), for the country as a whole, and for the regime they embodied. A failure in *peace*-making is today's highest political risk.

NOTES

An early version of this article appears in Peace and Change *Vol. 20 (Thousand Oaks: Sage Publications, 1995).*

1. On trading versus military, territorially-oriented states, see Richard Rosecrance, *The Rise of the Trading State* (New York: Basic Books, 1986).

2. I include groups like Egypt's Socialist Labor Party and Syria's Communist Party among the nationalists.

3. For a more detailed discussion of the coalitional politics in Israel and the Arab world, and of the implications for security postures, see Etel Solingen, "The Political Economy of Nuclear Restraint," *International Security* 19:2 (Fall, 1994), and idem. "The Domestic Sources of Regional Regimes: The Evolution of Nuclear Ambiguity in the Middle East," *International Studies Quarterly*, 38:2 (June, 1984).

4. For comprehensive overviews of arms control in the region, see Geoffrey Kemp, *The Control of the Middle East Arms Race* (Washington, DC: Carnegie Endowment for International Peace, 1991) and Alan Platt, ed., *Arms Control and Confidence-Building in the Middle East* (Washington, DC: United States Institute of Peace, 1992).

5. On the need to give priority to the nuclear issue, see Mohamed Nabil Fahmy, "Egypt's Disarmament Initiative," *The Bulletin of the Atomic Scientists*, 46:9 (November, 1990) and Mahmoud Karem, *A Nuclear-Weapon-Free Zone in the Middle East—Problems and Prospects* (Westport, CT: Greenwood Press, 1988).

6. See Shalhevet Freier, "A Nuclear-Weapon-Free-Zone in the Middle East and its Ambience," Washington Institute for Near East Policy, 1993.

7. Quoted in *Spector*, 1990, 208.

8. Interview distributed by the official Iranian news agency, quoted in R. Jeffry Smith, "Officials Say Iran is Seeking Nuclear Weapons Capability," *Washington Post*, October 30, 1991, A1. On the Iranian leadership's Manichean view of the world and the implications for nuclear

policy, see Akbar Etemed, "Iran," in Harald Mueller, ed., *A European Non-Proliferation Policy* (Oxford: Clarendon Press, 1987).

9. Pervez Hoodbhoy, "Myth-Building: The Islamic Bomb," *Bulletin of the Atomic Scientists*, June, 1993.

10. On two-level bargaining, played out on domestic and international levels, see Robert Putnam, "Diplomacy and Domestic Politics: The Logic of Two-Level Games," *International Organization*, 42:3 (Summer, 1988).

11. For example, see James Leonard, "Steps Toward a Middle East Free from Nuclear Weapons," *Arms Control Today*, April, 1991.

12. Yezid Sayigh, "Middle Eastern Stability and the Proliferation of Weapons of Mass Destruction," in Efraim Karsh, M.S. Navias, and P. Sabin, eds., *Non-Conventional Weapons Proliferation in the Middle East* (Oxford: Clarendon Press, 1993), 200.

13. See Ibrahim Karawan, "Monarchs, Mullahs, and Marshals: Islamic Regimes," *Annals of the American Academy of Political and Social Science* 524, 1992.

14. On economic liberalization in Syria, see Steven Heydemann, "Taxation Without Representation: Authoritarianism and Economic Liberalization in Syria," in Ellis Goldberg, Resat Kasaba, and Joel Migdal, eds., *Rules and Rights in the Middle East* (Seattle: University of Washington Press, 1993).

15. Lawson emphasizes the positive rewards of Assad's policies for large-scale commercial and agricultural groups. However, these groups surely assess their actual gains against those that might accrue from broader economic reform. See Fred Lawson, "Domestic Transformation and Foreign Steadfastness in Contemporary Syria," *Middle East Journal*, 48:1 (Winter, 1994).

16. Yehoshafat Harkabi, "Can War Still be an Instrument of Policy?" unpublished paper prepared for the Japan Foundation Center for Global Partnership, Symposium on "The End of the Century," September, 1993.

17. See Galia Golan, "A Palestinian State from an Israeli Point of View," paper presented at a UWM Conference on Race, Ethnicity, and Nationalism, October, 1993.

18. Asher Arian, *Israel and the Peace Process: Security and Political Attitudes in 1993* (Tel Aviv: Jaffee Center for Strategic Studies, Tel Aviv University, Memorandum No. 39, 1993).

19. Shalhevet Freier, "A Nuclear Weapon Free Zone in the Middle East and Its Ambience," Washington Institute for Near East Policy, 1993.

20. Opening session of the UCLA Conference on the Middle East Multilateral Peace Process, June, 1993.

21. For a formal analysis of the value of self-binding commitments, see Zeev Maoz and Dan Felsenthal, "Self-Binding Commitments, the Inducement of Trust, Social Choice, and the Theory of International Cooperation," *International Studies Quarterly*, 31:2 (June, 1987).

About the Editors

Steven L. Spiegel is a professor of political science at the University of California, Los Angeles. A specialist on policy issues in the Middle East, Dr. Spiegel is internationally recognized for organizing meetings among Arab, Israeli, and North American academics, policy analysts, scientists, and other experts on methods for furthering the Middle East peace process. Dr. Spiegel is the editor of *The Arab–Israeli Search for Peace* (1992) and *Conflict Management in the Middle East* (1992), coeditor (with Mark Heller and Jacob Goldberg) of *The Soviet–American Competition in the Middle East* (1988), author of the award-winning *The Other Arab–Israeli Conflict: Making America's Middle East Policy, from Truman to Reagan* and, most recently, author of *World Politics in a New Era*. His classic book of American foreign policy readings, *At Issue: Politics in the World Arena*, is in its seventh edition. His articles have appeared in *The National Interest, The New Republic*, *Commentary*, *Orbis, International Studies Quarterly, Middle East Insight*, and other publications, and he has made frequent appearances on "The Larry King Show" and National Public Radio.

David J. Pervin is a Ph.D. candidate at the Department of Political Science, University of California, Los Angeles, where he specializes in the international relations of the Middle East. With Steven L. Spiegel he is coeditor of *At Issue: Politics in the World Arena* (New York: St. Martin's Press, c.1994).

About the Contributors

M. Zuhair Diab is a strategic analyst and visiting research associate at the Department of War Studies, King's College, London, and a political analyst for BBC Radio and Television, ITN, Sky News, RTE Dublin, and National Public Radio and Television. He previously served with the Institute for Palestinian Studies (Beirut), then the Syrian Ministry of Foreign Affairs and as a strategic analyst at the Syrian National Security Bureau in Damascus. Among other works, Mr. Diab has contributed chapters and articles to *Regional Security in the Middle East: Arab and Israeli Concepts of Deterrence and Defense,* David Wurmser, ed., (forthcoming); *Middle East Policy; Israel at the Crossroads: the Challenge of Peace,* Efraim Karsh, ed.; *Brassey's Defense Yearbook 1993,* Centre for Defense Studies, ed.; *The Arab–Israeli Search for Peace in the Middle East,* Steven L. Spiegel, ed.; and *Yearbooks on Palestine: 1970, 1971, 1972* (Arabic), of which he was assistant editor.

Major General Ahmed Fakhr is director of the National Center for Middle East Studies in Cairo. He is a member of the Egyptian delegation to the multilateral negotiation for Middle East Arms Control and Regional Security and also chairman of the Popular Local Council of the Cairo Governate.

Mark Heller has been a senior research associate at the Jaffe Center for Strategic Studies in Tel Aviv since 1979. His many writings on the Middle East include *The Changing Dynamics of Soviet Policy in the Middle East: Between Old Thinking and New; No Trumpets, No Drums: A Two-State Settlement of the Israeli–Palestinian Conflict* (with Sari Nusseibeh); and *A Palestinian State: The Implications for Israel*. He edited and coauthored *The Middle East Military Balance* from 1983 to 1985 and coedited *The Soviet–American Competition in the Middle East,* with Steven L. Spiegel and Jacob Goldberg.

Michael D. Intriligator is professor of economics and political science at the University of California, Los Angeles, where he is also director of the Jacob Marschak Interdisciplinary Colloquium on Mathematics in the Behavioral Sciences. In the international arena, he has been president of the Peace Science Society and a member of the Council on Foreign Relations and the International Institute for Strategic Studies. Dr. Intriligator has coedited numerous works in the field of military strategy and arms control, including *Cooperative Models in International Relations Research; Strategies for Managing Nuclear Proliferation: Economic and Political Issues; East–West Relations: Elite Perceptions and Political Options,* and other works. Also a prolific author in the fields of economic theory, mathematical economics, econometrics, and health economics, his *Mathematical Optimization and Economic Theory* is in its thirteenth printing.

Arian Pregenzer is a physicist and manager of the Verification and Monitoring Analysis department at Sandia National Laboratories, in which capacity she has established a Cooperative Monitoring Center (at Sandia) to facilitate technology use in regional confidence-building by international participants. Dr. Pregenzer has previously served as a technical advisor to the U.S. Department of Energy's Office of Arms Control, representing that agency at the multilateral chemical weapons negotiations at the Conference on Disarmament in Geneva.

Yezid Sayigh is assistant director at the Centre of International Studies at the University of Cambridge, and was a MacArthur Scholar and research fellow at St. Antony's College, Oxford University. Dr. Sayigh acted as an advisor to the Palestinian delegation at the bilateral Middle East peace talks; headed the Palestinian delegation to the multilateral working group for Arms Control and Regional security; and was a member of the Palestinian delegation at the talks on implementing the Gaza–Jericho agreement. His most recent publications are *Arab Military Industry: Capability, Performance, and Impact*; *Rejecting Defeat: The Beginnings of Armed Action in the West Bank and Gaza Strip, 1967*; and *Confronting the 1990s: Security in the Developing Countries*. His articles have appeared in academic and specialized journals including *International Affairs, Middle East Journal, Third World Quarterly, Survival, RUSI Journal, Maghreb–Mashreq, Politique Etrangere, Journal of Palestine Studies,* and *Merip Reports.*

Lawrence Scheinman is the assistant director for Nonproliferation and Regional Arms Control of the U.S. Arms Control and Disarmament Agency. He most recently served as counselor for Nonproliferation in the Department of Energy, on leave from his position as Professor of Government and associate director of the Peace Studies program at Cornell University. He has previously been a tenured member of the faculties of political science at the University of California, Los Angeles and the University of Michigan, and has served with the U.S. Energy Research and Development Administration, Department of State, and the International Atomic Energy Agency. He is a member of the Council on Foreign Relations, the Washington Council on Non-proliferation, the Advisory Committee of the Atlantic Council of the United States Non-proliferation Project., and the Bar of the State of New York. Dr. Scheinman's publications include *Atomic Energy Policy in France under the Fourth Republic, EURATOM: Nuclear Integration in Europe,* and numerous monographs. His more recent articles have appeared in *Arms Control Today, Security Dialogue, IAEA Bulletin,* and the *Cornell International Law Journal.*

Etel Solingen is an Institute on Global Conflict and Cooperation Faculty Fellow and assistant professor in the Department of Politics and Society at the University of California, Irvine. She was also an IGCC Postdoctoral Fellow at the University of California, Los Angeles. She has contributed to a number of edited collections and journals, including most recently *International Organization, Comparative Politics, International Studies Quarterly, and International Security.* Dr. Solingen also edited *Scientists and the State: Domestic Structures and the International Context* and is the author of *Industrial Policy, Technology, and International Bargaining: Designing Nuclear Industries in Argentina and Brazil.*

Gerald M. Steinberg is a professor and director of research in security and arms control at the BESA Center for Strategic Studies at Bar-Ilan University in Israel. He also serves as an arms control consultant and to the Israeli Foreign Ministry. Dr. Steinberg's publications include *Lost in Space: The Domestic Politics of the Strategic Defense Initiative,* and *Satellite Reconnaissance.* He is a contributor to numerous edited volumes, and his articles and commentary have appeared in *Armed Forces and Society, Survival, Security Dialogue, Orbis, The Journal of Strategic Studies.* He has also been a Middle East and Israeli policy news analyst for BBC Radio and Television, CNN, Israeli Radio and Television, Skynet, CNN, National Public Radio, and others.

John M. Taylor is manager of the National Security Policy Research Department at Sandia National Laboratories. He has previously served as the Science Advisor to the U.S. START delegation in Geneva, and as the DOE liaison to the U.S. State Department for the implementation of Iraqi cease-fire resolutions.

Abdullah Toukan is science adviser to His Majesty King Hussein of Jordan.

About the Institute on Global Conflict and Cooperation

The University of California Institute on Global Conflict and Cooperation (IGCC) was founded in 1983 as a multi-campus research unit serving the entire University of California (UC) system. The institute's purpose is to study the causes of international conflict and the opportunities to resolve it through international cooperation. During IGCC's first five years, research focused largely on the issue of averting nuclear war through arms control and confidence-building measures between the superpowers. Since then the research program has diversified to encompass several broad areas of inquiry: regional relations, international environmental policy, international relations theory, and most recently, the domestic sources of foreign policy.

IGCC serves as a liaison between the academic and policy communities, injecting fresh ideas into the policy process, establishing the intellectual foundations for effective policy-making in the post–Cold War environment, and providing opportunities and incentives for UC faculty and students to become involved in international policy debates. Scholars, researchers, government officials, and journalists from the United States and abroad participate in all IGCC projects, and IGCC's publications—books, policy papers, and a semiannual newsletter—are widely distributed to individuals and institutions around the world.

In addition to projects undertaken by the central office at UC San Diego, IGCC supports research, instructional programs, and public education throughout the UC system. The institute receives financial support from the Regents of the University of California and the state of California, and has been awarded grants by such foundations as Ford, MacArthur, Rockefeller, Sloan, W. Alton Jones, Ploughshares, the Carnegie Corporation, the Rockefeller Brothers Fund, the United States Institute of Peace, and The Pew Charitable Trusts.

Susan L. Shirk, a professor in UC San Diego's Graduate School of International Relations and Pacific Studies and in the Department of Political Science, was appointed director of IGCC in June 1992 after serving for a year as acting director. Former directors of the institute include John Gerard Ruggie (1989–1991), and Herbert F. York (1983–1989), who now serves as director emeritus.

Index